POWERFUL

GUIDING
COALITIONS

How to **Build** and **Sustain** the
Leadership Team in Your PLC at Work®

BILL HALL

Solution Tree | Press

555 North Morton Street
Bloomington, IN 47404
800.733.6786 (toll free) / 812.336.7700
FAX: 812.336.7790

email: info@SolutionTree.com
SolutionTree.com

Visit **go.SolutionTree.com/PLCbooks** to download the free reproducibles in this book.

Printed in the United States of America

Library of Congress Cataloging-in-Publication Data

Names: Hall, Bill (Educator), author.
Title: Powerful guiding coalitions : how to build and sustain the
  leadership team in your PLC at work / Bill Hall.
Other titles: How to build and sustain the leadership team in your
  professional learning community at work
Description: Bloomington, IN : Solution Tree Press, [2021] | Includes
  bibliographical references and index.
Identifiers: LCCN 2021035344 (print) | LCCN 2021035345 (ebook) | ISBN
  9781951075170 (Paperback) | ISBN 9781951075187 (eBook)
Subjects: LCSH: Professional learning communities. | School management and
  organization. | Educational leadership. | School improvement programs. |
  Group work in education. | Team learning approach in education. |
  Educational change.
Classification: LCC LB1731 .H187 2021 (print) | LCC LB1731 (ebook) | DDC
  371.3/6--dc23
LC record available at https://lccn.loc.gov/2021035344
LC ebook record available at https://lccn.loc.gov/2021035345

Solution Tree
Jeffrey C. Jones, CEO
Edmund M. Ackerman, President

Solution Tree Press
President and Publisher: Douglas M. Rife
Associate Publisher: Sarah Payne-Mills
Art Director: Rian Anderson
Managing Production Editor: Kendra Slayton
Copy Chief: Jessi Finn
Senior Production Editor: Suzanne Kraszewski
Content Development Specialist: Amy Rubenstein
Copy Editor: Jessi Finn
Proofreader: Elisabeth Abrams
Text and Cover Designer: Kelsey Hergül
Editorial Assistants: Sarah Ludwig and Elijah Oates

This book is dedicated to my wife, Carol; to my daughters, Heather and Stacey, who are fifth-generation teachers; to my grandchildren, Tyler, Casey, Charlotte, and Lilli; and to the memory of my mother, Eloise.

ACKNOWLEDGMENTS

This book came very close to never being written. During the initial proposal submission and review process, I underwent emergency coronary bypass surgery. Physically recovering from the surgery went smoothly; after several months, I was back to normal. However, during the recovery and rehabilitation period, my challenge was to refocus on the work that lay ahead. Getting back into the daily rhythm to write and dedicating my time and energy to putting the manuscript back on the front burner were more difficult than I expected. Enter critical friend and fellow Solution Tree associate and author Chris Jakicic. This book became a reality thanks to her frequent support, advice, and encouragement throughout the process. She was an email, a phone call, or a text away, and for that, I am grateful. Thank you, Chris.

As with any successful project, it takes many talented and dedicated people to create a final product. This book is no exception. I want to acknowledge everyone in the Solution Tree family for their support, assistance, and guidance throughout the production of this book. I want to specifically thank Jeff Jones, Douglas Rife, Sarah Payne-Mills, Claudia Wheatley, Amy Rubenstein, and Suzanne Kraszewski for helping me fulfill my dream to become a published Solution Tree author. Your professionalism, patience, and encouragement are deeply appreciated.

I want to acknowledge the scores of Solution Tree associates and PLC leaders across the United States and Canada whom I had the privilege of learning from through interviews, surveys, and conversations. Your stories, experiences, and responses helped to make the content relevant for practitioners. Special recognition goes to colleagues and friends Mike Mattos, Anthony Muhammad, Ken Williams, Brian Butler, and Bill Ferriter who helped me immensely in answering questions such as, "What advice can you give me on how to write a book?" and "How did you successfully create, use, and sustain your guiding coalition during your years as a building principal?"

Finally, I want to acknowledge Rick DuFour, Becky DuFour, Bob Eaker, Bill Murray, John Stinson, Ned Straehla, Richard DiPatri, and Leroy Berry. They are the mentors and colleagues who had the most profound impact on my personal and professional growth throughout my career. Each challenged me to think and learn beyond what I thought possible. I cherish the personal relationship I had with each one and could never thank them enough for the difference they made in my life. I became a better version of me thanks to their influence and impact.

Solution Tree Press would like to thank the following reviewers:

Kevin Buscemi
Principal
Oak Ridge Elementary School
Palos Hills, Illinois

Molly Capps
Principal
McDeeds Creek Elementary
Southern Pines, North Carolina

Jennifer Evans
Principal
Burnham School
Cicero, Illinois

Jed Kees
Principal
Onalaska Middle School
Onalaska, Wisconsin

Jarod Lambert
Principal
Bush Elementary School
Conroe, Texas

Shelley Neher
Assistant Principal
Red Hawk Elementary School
Erie, Colorado

Teresa Olague
Principal
Planz Elementary School
Bakersfield, California

Bo Ryan
Principal
Greater Hartford Academy of the Arts
Middle School
Hartford, Connecticut

Scott Spoede
Assistant Principal
Chipeta Elementary School
Grand Junction, Colorado

Dawn Vang
Assistant Principal
McDeeds Creek Elementary
Southern Pines, North Carolina

Steven Weber
Associate Superintendent for Teaching
  and Learning
Fayetteville Public Schools
Fayetteville, Arkansas

Visit **go.SolutionTree.com/PLCbooks** to
download the free reproducibles in this book.

TABLE OF CONTENTS

ABOUT THE AUTHOR

 **William B. Hall** served as a classroom teacher, assistant principal, and principal with Brevard Public Schools in Florida. As a teacher, Bill was recognized as Teacher of the Year at Sherwood Elementary School in Melbourne, Florida. As principal of Surfside Elementary School in Satellite Beach, he received the key to the city in recognition of his outstanding leadership and service to the students and community.

During the last half of his career, Bill served as the director of educational leadership and professional development for the district. His responsibilities included leading the district's leadership development initiatives, the principal and assistant principal preparation programs, and the implementation of Professional Learning Communities at Work® (PLCs at Work) in support of the district's instructional model. Under Bill's leadership, twenty-seven of Brevard County's eighty-five schools were recognized as PLC Model Schools by Solution Tree.

Bill served as a past president of the Florida Association for Staff Development (FASD), now Learning Forward Florida. For his years of service to FASD, he received its Distinguished Contribution Award. He also served on two national conference planning committees for Learning Forward and served as a member of Learning Forward's National Conference Program Planning Committee.

As a result of his district's success with the PLC process, he was invited to become a member of Solution Tree's year-long PLC at Work Leaders' Academy led by Rick DuFour, Bob Eaker, and Becky DuFour. It was during the academy that Bill developed an interest in the idea of using PLC as a means for creating leadership capacity and sustainability in schools and school districts. Upon completion of the academy, Bill became a Solution Tree associate.

For two consecutive years, Bill received the Seiji Horiuchi Memorial Award from the U.S. Jaycees in recognition of his contribution to the area of individual development while serving as Florida's state individual development chairman. He served as a U.S. Educator Delegate to China for the College Board and Hanban, the Office of Chinese Language Council International. He is a senior fellow of the Institute for Development of Educational Activities, /I/D/E/A/, Academy of Fellows.

Bill has had articles published in NSDC's *JSD*, the *National FORUM of Educational Administration and Supervision Journal*, *AllThingsPLC Magazine*, the *District Management Journal (DMJ)*, and the U.S. Jaycees' *FUTURE Magazine*.

Bill earned his bachelor's degree in English from Erskine College in South Carolina and his master's degree in administration and supervision from Nova Southeastern University in Florida.

To learn more about Bill, visit @wbhall_ on Twitter.

To book William B. Hall for professional development, contact pd@SolutionTree.com.

INTRODUCTION

"**D**o you have a cardboard box?" is the question that jump-started my career in school leadership with Brevard Public Schools in Brevard County, Florida. It eventually led me to become responsible for the professional learning and leadership development of over nine thousand employees in what was then the forty-third-largest school district in the United States, located on Florida's Space Coast.

In the mid-1970s, during my sixth year as a classroom teacher, I became a member of a local civic organization that provided its members with opportunities for personal growth and leadership development through service to others. Shortly after joining, I volunteered to be the awards chairman for one of our chapter's biggest events, the local Fourth of July parade. I had no real experience in leading anything in college or as a teacher, so I was anxious about taking on such a huge responsibility. One evening, I called the parade chairman to share my concerns and discuss my responsibilities. That's when he asked, "Do you have a cardboard box?"

I responded, "A cardboard box? Uh, yes, I do."

"Well then," he replied, "take it down to the trophy shop; pick up the trophies for the first-, second-, and third-place parade unit winners; put them in the box; and bring them to the viewing stands on the morning of the parade."

"That's it?" I asked.

The chairman responded, "That's it."

With those words, the parade chairman provided me with key insight into the concept of leadership.

The Cardboard Box Theory

Contrary to what I believed, leadership doesn't have to be about huge projects costing millions of dollars and involving hundreds or thousands of people and extraordinarily high levels of risk. Leadership, particularly school leadership, can be found in day-to-day interactions with others. Leadership is embedded in the relationships school leaders have with students, teachers, parents, and the community. It is reflected in how leaders speak to and treat support personnel, vendors, and business partners. There are many examples of effective school leadership within a school leader's daily routine. They can take very little effort—like filling a cardboard box with trophies and delivering them to the right place at the right time—yet have an immense impact.

That simple realization about leadership gave me the confidence to lead at higher levels in the organization and take on more responsibility at school and ultimately in the district. These experiences eventually led to my appointment as assistant principal, principal, and director of educational leadership and professional development.

As the director of educational leadership, my primary responsibility was to develop school and district leaders. Throughout my district-level career, I focused on developing and growing leadership systemwide based on the cardboard box theory: *Keep it simple. Grow it slowly. Provide support and resources along the way. Focus on the personal and interpersonal levels, and the larger system components will benefit and strengthen.*

PLCs and Leadership Capacity

In 1993, during my second year as director, I attended a breakout session on school leadership at the annual National Staff Development Council (NSDC; now Learning Forward) conference. The presenter was Richard DuFour, then the superintendent of Adlai E. Stevenson High School in Lincolnshire, Illinois. His message on the foundation of school leadership was inspiring and thought provoking.

It was at this NSDC breakout session that I learned about the basic foundational practices that would become the PLC at Work process Rick and Robert Eaker would publish in their 1998 book *Professional Learning Communities at Work: Best Practices for Enhancing Student Achievement* (DuFour & Eaker, 1998). His message affirmed that following the cardboard box theory was possible in my new position. To create leadership development programs and processes for a large district, I should keep it simple, grow it slowly, focus on interpersonal skills, and learn all that I could about professional learning and its impact on student learning.

In early 1994, when planning for our district leadership team's summer charge session, we wanted to bring in an expert to spend a day working with our team of principals and district leaders. We needed an inspirational message on leadership that would engage and motivate our leadership team. I could think of no one better than Rick DuFour to deliver that message.

Rick kindly accepted our invitation to work with our leadership team that summer. What specifically caught our attention was his focus on what he referred to as the "three-legged stool," mission, vision, and values. Without realizing it at the time, our district was setting the stage for becoming a PLC-focused district. It would be several years after that leadership team presentation that I would cross paths again with Rick.

After that summer session, several schools in the district began their separate journeys to become more collaborative in their practice. They began by revising or developing their mission statements, creating their vision statements and embedding their vision into their school culture, and developing values (collective commitments) that established how staff members promised to behave when working with one another.

During the late 1990s, we had no formal leadership at the district level to launch our PLC initiative. However, several principals began to follow the development of the PLC process through articles in professional journals, through books authored by

Rick and Bob, and by attending professional learning sessions on the PLC process. As a result, a few schools began to experience positive results in the PLC work they were doing. Eventually, I began to witness the work of school-level leadership teams (guiding coalitions) and saw the promise these teams held in creating leadership capacity in our schools and within our district.

During the early 2000s, under the direction of a new superintendent, our district was getting ready to roll out a major organizational and cultural change initiative. For the first time, we were developing a districtwide mission, vision, and set of values to create a solid organizational foundation. Our professional development department was tasked to provide the professional development required for the yearlong effort. I immediately called Rick.

Rick returned to our district to share his message on creating the foundational components for a successful learning culture. He again addressed our district leadership team; but this time, in addition to updated and revamped underpinnings of the structural foundation of a PLC, he had a new and exciting message about school improvement, student learning, and leadership. He also had a new copresenter—Rebecca Burnette DuFour.

After working with Rick and Becky, the district developed a cultural foundation that led to almost a decade of unparalleled achievement and success. From my perspective, implementing the PLC processes had two distinct benefits: (1) collaborative teamwork benefited students and (2) working in collaborative teams introduced teachers to job-embedded leadership practices. It was then I became an advocate and champion of PLC at Work.

Through the implementation of PLC concepts, not only did student learning improve in our district; but the quality of teacher leadership and school-based leadership improved as well. As a result of our efforts to implement PLC processes, twenty-seven of our eighty-five schools became recognized as Model PLC schools (AllThingsPLC, n.d.).

What began as a journey based on a simple theory of slowly taking steps and providing support and resources along the way while focusing on personal and interpersonal relationships became an incredibly powerful process for creating and developing leadership capacity in our district. The key to our success was principal leadership and the creation of powerful school-based guiding coalitions.

When the task that lies ahead seems daunting and challenging, stop, take a breath, and ask yourself, "Where is my cardboard box?"

Leadership at All Levels

The leadership development programs and practices in our district flowed up from the leadership work being done at the school level. PLCs became the resource that created tremendous leadership capacity to fill our future leadership needs. By focusing our resources on developing school-level PLCs, our district was concurrently growing leadership at all levels. Building-level guiding coalitions became the training grounds that gave many teacher leaders opportunities to simultaneously lead and learn.

Job-embedded professional learning provided by school-based guiding coalitions became the mainstay and backbone of our leadership development initiatives. The district tapped into this tremendous leadership resource and developed a high-quality leadership development system that eventually created pools of qualified personnel to fill leadership vacancies in the system.

The Guiding Coalition

Leaders of the PLC process must begin by acknowledging that "no one person will have the energy, expertise, and influence to lead a complex change process until it becomes anchored in the organization's culture without first gaining the support of key staff members" (DuFour, DuFour, Eaker, Many, & Mattos, 2016, p. 27). Mike Mattos, Richard DuFour, Rebecca DuFour, Robert Eaker, and Thomas W. Many (2016) define a *guiding coalition* as:

> An alliance of key members of an organization who are specifically charged with leading a change process through predictable turmoil. Members of the coalition should include opinion leaders—people who are so respected within the organization that others are likely to follow their lead. (p. 21)

The guiding coalition is the lead team or the model collaborative team in a PLC. This team is the center of a school's leadership universe from which leadership opportunities, leadership development, and leadership experiences radiate. Ultimately, every staff member in a PLC assumes leadership responsibilities, but it is the guiding coalition that sets the tone for the collaborative work done throughout the school.

A Powerful Guiding Coalition

While having a guiding coalition is critical, every PLC should aim to ultimately build a *powerful* guiding coalition. This power does not come from a title, authority, or position; it is not power over anyone or anything. Powerful guiding coalitions release the leadership potential within the team.

John Kotter (1999) identifies eight errors organizations make when attempting to transform; the second error, according to Kotter, is "not creating a powerful enough guiding coalition" (p. 79). Kotter (1999) suggests the following actions are required to ensure your guiding coalition is powerful enough to recognize and release its leadership potential:

- Assemble a guiding coalition that is composed of the right people.
- Ensure that your guiding coalition operates with high levels of trust among its members.
- Create and pursue a common goal shared by the members of your guiding coalition.

Kotter (1996) further states that:

> The resulting guiding coalition will have the capacity to make needed change happen despite all the forces of inertia. It will have the potential, at least, to do the hard work involved in creating the necessary vision, communicating the vision widely, empowering a broad base of people to take action, ensuring credibility, building short-term wins, leading and managing dozens of different change projects, and anchoring the new approaches in the organization's culture. (pp. 65–66)

Your goal is not to merely assemble a team of leaders that will advise and assist you and change the name of that team to *guiding coalition*. The purpose of this book is to propel your school's leadership capacity to far greater heights. Putting together a leadership team is like dipping your toes into the shallow end of the leadership pool. Taking that simple guiding coalition and making it *powerful* is the primary focus of this book! After reading this book and after putting into place the research-based concepts and processes outlined in the following chapters, you and your guiding coalition will be diving from the high platform into the deep end of the leadership pool!

Every employee in a school, regardless of position, length of experience, job responsibilities, and so on, has a professional obligation to help steer the direction of the school. The role of the guiding coalition is to lead and model how employees can fulfill their obligation to contribute in some way to leading the school.

In a PLC, the actions for substantial school transformation are guided by a powerful team of individuals who have the commitment, desire, willingness, and skills to lead the school through the change process. This team is responsible for helping, advising, and supporting the principal and staff as the school moves from a culture that values isolation and less effective practices to one that honors and values collaboration and puts students first. The primary focus of this team is to embed PLC concepts and practices into the school culture. Such a focus results in continuous improvement and higher levels of student learning.

The School Leader

The responsibilities on a school leader's shoulders can be overwhelming. The leadership role is extraordinarily critical if schools are to develop as successful PLCs. Principals must formally and purposefully create, develop, and lead a powerful guiding coalition within their school. This leadership cannot be delegated, assigned, or subordinated. Principals cannot effectively lead from afar or by proxy. PLCs require committed and actively involved leadership. When a principal establishes and maintains a powerful guiding coalition, collaboration becomes the cultural expectation for every member of every team in the school.

Although the focus of this book is powerful guiding coalitions, they do not exist in a vacuum; they do not and cannot stand on their own. They connect to the much larger community of leadership. This book examines how the powerful guiding coalitions in

PLCs have the potential and capacity to positively impact the leadership of schools and districts.

About This Book

This book explores what it means to be a powerful guiding coalition—and how to create such a team, develop it, and sustain it. This book is a resource for schools beginning their journey to becoming a PLC, those already on the path, and schools looking to get back on track. It is a guide for principals and other school leaders, as well as a resource for members of a guiding coalition.

This book is not meant to stand alone as the definitive resource on developing and sustaining leadership capacity for PLCs. It is meant to be a part of your professional learning library to support and complement other books and resources related to PLCs. These resources could include, but are not limited to, *Learning by Doing: A Handbook for Professional Learning Communities at Work®, Third Edition* (DuFour et al., 2016); *Concise Answers to Frequently Asked Questions About Professional Learning Communities at Work®* (Mattos et al., 2016); *Revisiting Professional Learning Communities at Work®: Proven Insights for Sustained, Substantive School Improvement, Second Edition* (DuFour, DuFour, Eaker, Mattos, & Muhammad, 2021); and *Leading PLCs at Work® Districtwide: From Boardroom to Classroom* (Eaker, Hagadone, Keating, & Rhoades, 2021). Additional resources that may prove valuable in supporting your teams along the PLC journey include the AllThingsPLC website (allthingsplc.info) and *AllThingsPLC Magazine*.

Chapters

Chapter 1 defines what a guiding coalition is and why having one is important. Your school most likely has an administrative team or leadership team currently in place. This chapter explores the differences between having a team to generally lead the school and building a guiding coalition to specifically lead the PLC process. Your guiding coalition is the team to which all other teams in your school look as the model of appropriate behavior. Members of the guiding coalition learn and practice skills and share ideas that transfer to leading their grade-level or department teams. In this chapter, you will study the makeup of your team and what the members' roles and responsibilities should be.

Chapter 2 emphasizes the importance of learning, understanding, and leading the PLC basics. As your guiding coalition moves your school along its PLC journey, it will view the basic PLC concepts of the three big ideas and the four critical questions through a leadership lens. Working through those concepts at the leadership level will facilitate and reinforce effective implementation at the collaborative team level.

Chapter 3 reviews three basic school structures so that you can ensure the foundation of your PLC is solidly in place before your guiding coalition moves to higher levels of responsibility. This chapter reinforces that only the whole school can be called a PLC—a community of professionals learning together.

Chapter 4 explores the importance of building and maintaining powerful relationships. Education is a people-intensive profession. School leaders are obligated to faithfully and consistently ensure that relationships with students, employees, parents, and the community are positive, professional, and sensitive to the various needs of these groups. This chapter examines the importance that trust and empowerment have in building powerful relationships.

Chapter 5 looks at leading the guiding coalition. Collaborative leadership can be an effective and efficient way to move grade-level and department teams toward higher levels of collaboration. Teams are made of unique individuals. Team members have different needs, gifts, ideas, and goals. Harnessing the power of a large group of individuals can be challenging. However, by meeting the basic needs of different individual styles, and by drawing from their strengths, guiding coalition members will be able to confidently lead their own collaborative learning teams.

Chapter 6 introduces the idea of leadership levers to help reduce the amount of leadership effort required of school leaders. These PLC leadership levers can multiply, enhance, or strengthen your leadership. Applying these levers can create a powerful, synergistic school culture. This chapter will challenge you and your guiding coalition to identify processes and practices currently in place to determine your school's strengths and its opportunities for improvement. As you look at each lever, you will want to ask yourself, "Are we applying this specific PLC leadership lever (leading the learning, harnessing the power of teacher leadership, and so on)? If so, how do we celebrate and recognize teams and individuals who embrace and contribute to using this particular leadership lever? If not, why is it not in place, and what can our guiding coalition do to introduce or strengthen this lever?"

Finally, the epilogue is a call to action to bring to life the concepts this book explores. It will challenge you and your guiding coalition to look in the mirror and assess what effective practices are in place to support and move forward your PLC efforts and identify potential gaps or disparities in PLC processes.

Next Steps, FAQs, Reflections, and Voices From the Field

Each chapter includes next steps for consideration and frequently asked questions (FAQs). The FAQs and responses are compiled from personal interviews and survey responses of more than eighty PLC leaders from across the Unites States and Canada who have experienced and led successful PLC practices and processes. Next steps and FAQs were also gleaned from reviewer comments given during the writing process. These questions reveal real-world concerns and problems that require practical, real-world solutions. Guiding coalitions will face many challenges and barriers. The FAQs segment at the end of each chapter provides you with insight into potential hurdles, which practitioners have experienced when leading PLCs. The solutions offered provide awareness into how PLC leaders approach common roadblocks to their PLC efforts.

The end of each chapter contains a reflection component. This reflective piece is designed for you and your guiding coalition to process PLC concepts at a personal level. Throughout this book, you will find Voices From the Field features from school leaders, administrators, and other education professionals who have successfully led high-performing PLCs. These exemplary PLC leaders share their personal insights and key learnings on leading through their guiding coalitions.

From Current Practice to Best Practice

Becoming a PLC demands significant changes to your school's organization, structure, and processes. Schools and districts have a path to follow for undertaking PLC transformation. School leaders must clearly understand PLC terms, definitions, and concepts before introducing them to the rest of the staff. PLC culture building must precede PLC foundation building. The process takes time, patience, and commitment. Implementing PLC concepts and transforming school culture are complex work.

As a school leader, you can begin steering your school from current practice to best practice. Best practice leads schools toward collaboration, continuous improvement, and high levels of learning for all, for students and staff alike. The building principal is who leads change of this scope, complexity, and magnitude. Period.

Leading today's schools is far too complicated and difficult for individual principals to carry the entire leadership burden. School leadership job descriptions often seem to require nothing short of superpowers for principals to perform the listed duties and responsibilities. Conditions such as lack of access to support, high job complexity, and lack of time needed to complete all necessary activities contribute to school leaders leaving their positions (Levin & Bradley, n.d.). When leaders have these worries added to their already full plates, especially in lower-performing schools, it is no surprise that even the most talented and experienced principals may choose to leave. Even in perfect conditions, leadership is a challenging endeavor.

To best meet the many challenges that you and your staff face, you will want to surround yourself with the best people who will support and advise you along your journey of improved student learning for all. By distributing leadership responsibilities to your staff through your guiding coalition, the crushing weight of mandates, initiatives, and administrivia can be lessened. Viewing your leadership actions through the cardboard box theory based on simplicity, slow growth, and support through interpersonal connections may very well make your ascent to the highest levels of leadership possible.

CHAPTER 1

CREATING A POWERFUL GUIDING COALITION

If you want to go quickly, go alone.
If you want to go far, go together.

—African proverb

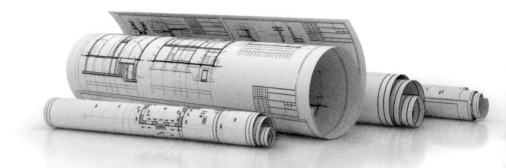

Having a guiding coalition is not just a good idea or a suggestion—it is a crucial step in becoming a PLC. There is consistency among thought leaders that having a guiding coalition is mandatory (Keating, Eaker, DuFour, & DuFour, 2008). According to the Wallace Foundation (2013):

> A broad and longstanding consensus in leadership theory holds that leaders in all walks of life and all kinds of organizations, public and private, need to depend on others to accomplish the group's purpose and need to encourage the development of leadership across the organization. (p. 9)

As noted in the introduction, a guiding coalition is an alliance of staff from within a school who have the responsibility of leading a change process through the many challenges and barriers of implementation. Guiding coalitions should include people who are leaders and allies within the school. Members of a guiding coalition work together to achieve common goals and guide collaborative teacher teams as they implement PLC cycles of continuous improvement (Mattos et al., 2016).

Without a formal guiding coalition, successful implementation of key PLC concepts will be very difficult, if not impossible. Anthony Muhammad notes that one person cannot transform a school's culture or dictate a school's mission (A. Muhammad, personal communication, June 2, 2021). Austin Buffum, Mike Mattos, and Chris Weber (2012) recommend that schools create a guiding coalition to lead the change process. They note:

> This guiding coalition is not the school "dictatorship committee" but a team that learns deeply about best practices, assesses candidly the school's current reality, determines potential next steps to improve the school,

identifies possible obstacles and points of leverage, and plans the best way to create staff consensus and ownership. (Buffum et al., 2012, p. 20)

This team that leads the change process includes members who become key in all improvement efforts, are open and prepared to move into leadership roles, and are willing to make more public their own practices as they lead colleagues in the work of PLC transformation (Wilhelm, 2017). Becoming a PLC is a significant cultural change. The guiding coalition is the team that leads that change initiative in a school. The guiding coalition focuses on continuous improvement and supports the collaborative teams charged with ensuring high levels of learning for all students (Martin & Rains, 2018; Muhammad & Cruz, 2019).

The guiding coalition is the model team for all collaborative teams within a school to emulate. Its most essential responsibility is to ensure organizational and cultural changes lead to the creation of a true PLC structure built on the foundation of mission, vision, values (collective commitments), and goals (DuFour et al., 2016).

Why Create a Guiding Coalition?

"Senior leaders cannot implement change alone. They need partners in responsible leadership positions who have organizational expertise and credibility to work with them" (Tanner, 2021).

A focused guiding coalition is critical "to establish credibility, practice empathy, and initiate change with the necessary support for educators to succeed" (Muhammad & Cruz, 2019, p. 120).

"A powerful, enthusiastic team of volunteers from across an organization . . . is a crucial tool for leaders looking to put new strategies into effect and transform their organizations. And deciding who should take part in the guiding coalition is essential" (Goin, 2012).

"Put simply, the guiding coalition is an easy notion to grasp, but surprisingly hard to do well. Yet the success of a change [program] hinges first and foremost on the quality of the team that guides it. As a consequence, the composition, alignment and coordination of this guiding coalition is key. A misaligned, ill-fitting, uncaring team can cause the entire [program] to flounder or grind to a halt" (Ferrabee, 2016).

"Building a guiding coalition to facilitate the change management process is an essential step that can make or break change initiatives" (Doseck, 2015).

"[Change] requires a team of people powerful and accountable enough to give credibility to the fact that the change is essential. This team, which we call a guiding coalition, must have the right composition, level of trust, and a shared objective . . . [to drive] the process. And by that I mean a group of people . . . who learn to work as a team and then take on, in a sense 'guiding,' all of the other steps that are necessary to make something big happen" (Kotter, 2011).

Traditional Leadership Teams

If you are new to the PLC process, you might say to yourself, "I already have a leadership team." Indeed, traditional schools use formal and informal teams to serve many functions. Traditional administrative teams are typically made up of school principals, assistant principals, administrators, and deans, along with some support personnel on an as-needed basis, like guidance counselors, academic specialists, instructional coaches, or school resource officers. They typically deal with issues, problems, and tasks that are highly confidential and sensitive. In many cases, these small, select teams deal with applying board policy or state or provincial law. Administrative teams may address employee-related issues, including employee discipline, evaluation, and termination, and the most serious or confidential student issues. These teams may work with the district's security office, its human resources office, law enforcement agencies at all levels, or perhaps state or provincial department of education personnel. Most conversations that administrative teams conduct occur behind closed doors.

Teams that do not require administrator attendance may lead select school-improvement initiatives, or they may pursue grade-level goals, content-specific goals, or other objectives that are not schoolwide. Specific teams may be permanent while others are temporary, depending on their roles, responsibilities, and purposes. Some teams, such as ad hoc committees, serve a specific purpose and have a shelf life that ends after their responsibilities are completed or their goals are met.

Many schools have some type of leadership team whose members serve in an advisory capacity but do not necessarily lead in a formal sense. Other schools may have a leadership team that discusses a wide variety of issues, programs, initiatives, and goals. This more traditional leadership team may focus on every aspect of the school, from discipline in the common areas to the traffic pattern in the car loop, to the implementation of a newly adopted reading series, to the location of a new mural of the school's mascot. This team may advise the administration on some issues and have involvement in the actual decision-making process on other topics. Members of this leadership team might include the principal, the assistant principal, and a representative from every grade level or department, including a representative for activity teachers, exceptional education (special education) teachers, and other specialists.

The traditional leadership team tends to provide top-down administrators with a way to share information and receive all teachers' input on many topics through select grade-level or department representatives. Leading schools exclusively through teacher representatives has a few drawbacks. Not all teachers on staff feel a personal connection with the leaders of their school. Representatives generally share information between the teachers they represent and administrators according to their understanding or interpretation of that information; therefore, not all grade levels or departments receive the same message or the same content. Leading exclusively through representation tends to raise more questions than answers. The traditional representation model may focus more on managerial tasks like meeting deadlines, creating and following schedules, and allocating resources. While important, overemphasis on these tasks keeps leaders from focusing on student and staff learning, creating a more collaborative culture, and school improvement. This type of leadership structure generally concentrates on things, not people.

Just as no principal can lead a school single-handedly, a school leadership team cannot lead every program, every facility issue, or every process on campus. To add leading a complex change initiative, like becoming a PLC, to an already burdened team's responsibilities would certainly result in team overload. A leadership team that is involved with every aspect of the school ultimately ends up as a team of jacks-of-all-trades and masters of none. Unless a traditional leadership team is composed of the right people focused on the correct work and basing all decisions on best practice, chances are excellent that personal opinions and self-interests, rather than a focus on student learning, will eventually drive the team's actions and decisions.

Table 1.1 shows the differences between traditional leadership teams and guiding coalitions in a PLC.

The PLC Leadership Team

The team that formally leads its school toward becoming a PLC can be called different names. It might be referred to as an *action team, teacher leadership team, administrative team, school-improvement team, design team, data team,* or *executive team.* The architects of the PLC at Work process call this team the *guiding coalition* (DuFour et al., 2016). But it does not matter what you call the team that leads your PLC; what is critical is what the team does.

Whatever you call this team, your grade-level or department collaborative teams must understand this team is leading the PLC process. Collaborative teams must know what the guiding coalition's specific purpose is and how its duties and responsibilities differ from those of all other teams on campus. Guiding coalitions are very different from traditional school leadership teams.

Your school's guiding coalition should model the structure and processes required of the collaborative teams within your PLC. Grade-level and departmental collaborative teams that are structured like, act like, and sound like the guiding coalition have an excellent chance of staying true to PLC concepts. A leadership team cannot have behaviors or expectations of its own responsibilities that differ from the behaviors and expectations of the teams it leads.

Guiding coalitions in PLCs are tasked with achieving the following goals.

- Become PLC experts by learning about the PLC process—from common vocabulary to the cycle of continuous improvement in which collaborative teacher teams participate.

- Become experts on the PLC process's benefits for students, teachers, and the school community.

- Disseminate information about the PLC process to collaborative teacher teams.

Table 1.1: Leadership Teams Versus Guiding Coalitions

	Leadership Team	Guiding Coalition
Responsibilities	This team is responsible for leading multiple areas of the school, such as facilities, student discipline, school improvement, community relations, the PLC initiative or processes, and so on.	This team is singularly responsible for leading PLC processes at the school. It does not lead any competing initiatives at the school.
Member selection	Team members are selected (or volunteer) using criteria such as their longevity in their position, their specific knowledge or experience in multiple school-related topics, and their need or willingness to gain school-level leadership experiences. They might be handpicked by the principal, or they might gain membership, regardless of whether they meet any of the aforementioned criteria, if they are the only people available.	Team members might be selected using stricter criteria based on leadership, position power, expertise, reputation, relationships, and credibility (Kotter, 1999). Members may be voted onto the team by peers, handpicked by the principal, selected through an application process, and so on.
Focus	Team members may assist and support the principal in making decisions about multiple areas and topics. The team may have limited responsibility to focus on a narrow aspect of the school (such as current issues facing the school, public relations, communications, celebrations, staff morale, and so on).	Team members spend their entire meeting time on leading the PLC. The team primarily focuses on student learning, a collaborative culture, and results.
Decision-making authority	Team members may advise the principal or give their opinions and thoughts about issues and concerns, but they may not be formally involved in the actual decision-making process.	Team members serve to advise and support the principal and share as equals in the decision-making process.
Membership	Administrative personnel may be the only members of the team for confidentiality, personnel, and discipline purposes. Other aspects of the school might be led by ad hoc committees or department or grade-level teams.	The team usually has members who share high levels of trust, share a common goal, and are considered opinion leaders who are so respected that others will likely follow their lead.
Organizational structure	The team may have a leadership hierarchy where administrators have more of a boss relationship with the rest of the team. The members may have a tendency to operate by the credo, "Do as we say, not as we do."	The team has a flat organizational structure. There is no position of power. All team members sit as equals on the guiding coalition. The motto of this team might be, "We will model the way for how all teams will operate."
Decision-making options	The team may make decisions in several ways: decide and announce, seek input from a sampling of team members and then decide, seek input from the entire team and then decide, reach consensus, or delegate the decision with criteria or constraints (Interaction Associates, n.d.).	The team makes decisions preferably by consensus notwithstanding unusual circumstances. When they cannot reach consensus in a timely manner, the principal has the fallback decision-making option to gather input from the team and decide (Interaction Associates, n.d.).

- Lead PLC transformation by example; maintain a laser-like concentration on improving student learning, focusing on results, and working collaboratively.
- Model continuous improvement.
- Design job-embedded learning opportunities.
- Support collaborative teacher teams.

For schools that are just beginning their transformation, the guiding coalition is instrumental in leveraging buy-in from faculty and staff. DuFour and his colleagues (2016) identify building a guiding coalition as a first step to take when beginning the PLC journey. By working closely, the guiding coalition creates trust and promotes buy-in by introducing foundational PLC elements. For example, creating and using team norms for the guiding coalition set the tone of cultural expectations that will be made of all collaborative teams. Also, creating and monitoring organizational values help create higher levels of trust. As the principal introduces and implements each PLC element with the guiding coalition, team members have the opportunity to increase their buy-in and ownership of PLC processes. Once the guiding coalition assumes ownership of these concepts, team members will be more likely to pass their buy-in on to the members of their collaborative learning teams.

Be cautioned, however, that the mere creation of a guiding coalition is not enough to lead the difficult and challenging work of PLC transformation. Should the wrong people be on the team, should the team's assignment be in name only, or should the team end up being one of "do as we say, not as we do," the movement needed to lead your PLC will come to a screeching halt. Creating a guiding coalition is one thing. Creating a *powerful* guiding coalition is something else entirely.

Organization of Teams for PLC Implementation

As principals begin to transform their schools' culture into that of a PLC, it is mandatory they ask, "Who before what?" (Collins, 2001). By asking "Who?" first, principals are taking the first steps to creating the critical mass of professionals, the guiding coalition, who will help them lead the PLC process. When principals ask "What?" (formation of the PLC) first, they could easily become overwhelmed and frustrated for fear that they must lead the entire process single-handedly. Identifying the who relieves the anxiety because there is comfort in knowing others will assist in moving the process forward. Principals who try to lead the change process by themselves will easily tire and become frustrated as they attempt to answer every question, defend every decision, and individually convince a school full of staff members that becoming a PLC is the way to increase student achievement. The guiding coalition is the single most powerful device for moving schools to the highest level of effectiveness.

In his book *Good to Great: Why Some Companies Make the Leap . . . and Others Don't*, Jim Collins (2001) equates leading the transformation process to organizing a bus ride for your school personnel. Your school, your PLC, is your bus. Your challenge is to place all personnel, certificated and noncertificated, on the bus and in the right seats. He also suggests getting the wrong people off the bus.

Imagine an empty bus. The first seat—the driver's seat—is the easiest to fill. This seat is the principal's seat and has your name on it, so slide in. Collins (2001) suggests that your next step would be to seat your guiding coalition members. To fill the guiding coalition seats, select one member from each grade level or department. If you are the principal of a large high school, your guiding coalition would have too many members if one representative for every course sat on your team. A better idea would be to have the department heads (for example, the heads of mathematics, science, social studies, English, foreign languages, and so on) on your guiding coalition and have people other than the department heads lead course-level collaborative teams (for example, an algebra I team, an algebra II team, a geometry team, and so on).

The guiding coalition sits in two areas of the bus. When the guiding coalition meets, the members sit in the seats at the front of the bus near your seat. When the team is not meeting, guiding coalition members sit with their grade-level, department-level, or course-level teams in seats scattered throughout the bus. The principal or administrative team creates the teams; the guiding coalition may assist. An important goal in identifying who is on what team is to ensure all staff members are on a meaningful team—a team on which their membership makes the most sense. To create meaningful teams, the principal may consider input from the individual staff member, from the guiding coalition, and from members of the teams impacted. Some schools include noncertificated or support personnel on their guiding coalitions.

Once your grade-level or department-level team leaders are in their seats, the teaching staff take their collaborative team seats. Specialists and activity teachers will join the appropriate collaborative team to which they are assigned. All certificated staff should now be on your bus.

Finally, the leaders of your support services, head custodian, cafeteria manager, administrative assistant, child care coordinator, and so on will take their seats. Once these managers and supervisors are seated, all support personnel join them.

Collins (2001) and his team initially assumed that organizations successfully lead transformation by setting their vision, direction, and strategies first and then getting employees to commit to the new focus and adjust to the new course set by management. To their surprise, they learned that great organizations do quite the opposite. Great organizations identify self-motivated employees who have the initiative to help their companies attain levels of success that they have never experienced. By identifying the employees (the who) first, the what (direction) becomes less relevant because the selected employees will adapt and adjust to whatever direction the organization declares important and critical to the mission. Great organizations do not first identify where their bus is going and then get people on the bus. Why? Because no sooner does the bus start the journey than leadership decides the route needs to change. Examples of such change could be in the form of a change in leadership at the district or board level, a change in district, state, or provincial mandates, or a change in resources. When changes in the direction of the bus are made, the organization now has a bus filled with people who are not interested in going in the new direction (Collins, 2001).

To create and build a great PLC, principals should ensure they understand the following three key points from Collins's research (Diplo Learning Corner, 2015).

1. To more easily transform your school's structure, processes, and culture, start with the who rather than the what.

2. Get the right people on the bus and in the right seats. Doing so will eliminate potential problems motivating and managing your team. The right people will be self-motivated to create great results.

3. If your school follows the right direction (its mission and vision), but has the wrong people in the wrong seats, your PLC will not reach its potential.

To get the right passengers on the bus and in the right seats, as principal, you must first determine the who. Think of the committed, motivated, excited, flexible, roll-up-their-sleeves-and-get-to-work people on your staff who have the interest and desire to do whatever it takes to ensure that every student on your campus—whether it's brick and mortar, virtual, or otherwise—learns and succeeds. They are your "glass half-full" staff members. They turn lemons into lemonade. These individuals should make up the majority of your guiding coalition. Once on the guiding coalition, these staff members will be willing and excited to go wherever the bus goes, even when it changes direction. They will help guide, steer, and lead your school to where it should go to become a PLC.

Guiding Coalition Membership

Once you understand why having a guiding coalition is a critical initial step to leading your PLC, you will want to answer the question, "Who will be on my guiding coalition?" This section will describe different criteria and characteristics that you may wish to consider when creating (or re-evaluating) the membership of your team.

Four Essential Types of Power

Principals should create a guiding coalition that includes four essential types of power (Buffum, Mattos, & Malone, 2018). These four types of power are (1) the power of position, (2) the power of expertise, (3) the power of credibility, and (4) the power of leadership ability.

1. **Power of position:** People can gain positional power through their formal authority based on the job title they possess, the office they occupy, the budget or personnel they oversee, or the place they hold on the school organization chart (Kotter, 1999). Your guiding coalition should have enough members with positional power that those not on the team will find it difficult to block the necessary work of the PLC.

2. **Power of expertise:** Expertise speaks to work ethic, discipline, work experiences, or knowledge of subject matter and processes (Kotter, 1996). Expertise required on the guiding coalition may include knowledge of and

experience with PLC processes and products. Someone who has been a member of a successful PLC in another school or district could be a valuable member of the guiding coalition.

3. **Power of credibility:** Guiding coalition members who are believable and who have solid reputations can help forward the change through their messaging and persuasion. Credible guiding coalition members are trustworthy, and other people take their messaging seriously (Buffum et al., 2012).

4. **Power of leadership ability:** To effectively lead the PLC process, guiding coalition members require leadership skills and management skills. Individuals with proven management experiences help structure and oversee the process while those with leadership experiences help drive and direct the work that will result in a sustained change in direction. Managers develop plans; leaders develop vision (Kotter, 1996).

Members of your guiding coalition may be strong in one type of power yet weak in the other three. Many times, guiding coalition members are strong in multiple types. It is rare to find personnel who are exceptionally strong in all four types. You will want to select a team that collectively has as much balance of these four types of power as possible.

Two Types of Members to Avoid

John Kotter (1996) recommends two types of people to avoid putting on your guiding coalition no matter what. The first type is individuals who have "egos that fill up a room, leaving no space for anybody else" (Kotter, 1996, p. 59). The second type is individuals who cause a sufficient amount of mistrust to destroy collaboration.

All organizations, including schools, are subject to having individuals with large egos. Some administrators and team leaders think so highly of themselves that little else matters to them. If these types of people are in essential leadership positions, Kotter (1996) warns that leaders can "kiss teamwork and a dramatic transformation goodbye" (p. 60).

Great leaders can be confident, positive, and self-assured without being egotistical. Such leaders know their liabilities and know how to match those vulnerabilities with the strengths and positive attributes of others. However, when leaders believe they are the heart and soul of their organization, it can have disastrous results.

The second type destroys trust. They talk about others behind their backs. They gossip. They violate confidentiality. They stir things up. They pit people against each other and spew their venom throughout the organization.

These types of people can be smart, driven, and effective to a degree. These attributes can allow them to move up the ladder to positions of increased responsibility and authority, including being placed in seats on the guiding coalition.

When creating your guiding coalition for the first time or when changing the makeup of your current leadership team, move slowly and deliberately. Be purposeful in your decision making, and most importantly, be transparent. Clearly communicate the purpose and the process of creating your guiding coalition to avoid having the team appear to be a group of your favorites or a collection of people who will always agree with you.

In business, guiding coalition members who are unproductive or who get in the way of progress can be buried deep in the organization. They run the risk of losing their positions on the guiding coalition or being transferred to the branch office in Greenland, where they are never heard from again.

In education, you have different challenges. Unlike some businesses where keeping a position is less secure, positions in education are more protected through contract language and state or provincial law. Generally, movement of business personnel is easier to accomplish than moving school personnel. For example, in business, a junior executive who is not the right fit on the guiding coalition can be removed from his position and moved to the office on the other side of the building or moved from the eleventh floor down to the third floor. Schools don't operate that way, nor should they. Just because an English teacher on the guiding coalition doesn't buy into the PLC concept of teacher collaboration doesn't mean he or she should be moved to another school or district. Just because some teachers are not a "good fit" for your guiding coalition does not mean they are not excellent classroom teachers.

Members you want to move off the current guiding coalition will still be in the building. As principal, you must consider several questions: Is it worth it to remove these people? How might they react? Could they possibly cause harm to your collaborative efforts? Since your district most likely has no schools in Greenland, can you provide unproductive or ill-suited team members with other leadership opportunities or responsibilities? Providing such opportunities might maintain a team member's self-esteem, take advantage of specific job skills in areas where he or she shines, or increase or improve his or her ability to collaborate with others in another area of the school. Pursuing such alternate opportunities could provide the very experiences a team member needs to become eligible to serve on the guiding coalition in the future. You must deal with such decisions on a case-by-case basis.

When you know potentially dangerous personalities might be considered for the guiding coalition or are on your current guiding coalition, keep them off or remove them at all costs. If their membership is unavoidable, keep a very close eye on them. There are times when keeping a toxic personality on the guiding coalition might be a better decision than removing him or her, such as if the toxic personality on your guiding coalition is the spouse of a school board member. In such a case, establishing your guiding coalition based on sound PLC concepts may be exactly what you need to not only keep that personality on your team, but perhaps lessen their toxic effect on others. This can be done through creation and implementation of team norms, protocols, and collective commitments for your PLC. By embedding norms and values into your school's culture, you have set the behavioral expectations for everyone on staff—even your most difficult personalities. They are helping define the behaviors they, too, are expected to live by. Through proper implementation and monitoring of these

PLC components, you will be better able to move from focusing on personalities to focusing on behaviors.

Five Types of Adopters

In his book *Diffusion of Innovations*, Everett M. Rogers (2003) identifies five categories of adopters that arise when an organization brings about change. The five adopter styles accept change differently, on a range from zealous acceptance of the change to strong resistance to the change.

Not all members of your faculty have the same motivation for adopting change or for making a substantive transformation like becoming a PLC. Of the five types, your guiding coalition will most likely come from the first two, innovators and early adopters. Most highly effective guiding coalition members will more than likely come from the early adopter category. This category includes the majority of influencers and opinion leaders who are best suited to lead and sustain your PLC transformation.

1. **Innovators** make up approximately 2.5 percent of an organization. They are attracted to change because it is something new and exciting. Innovators enjoy the exploration. They take risks and are willing to assume those risks even if they lead to failure (Pearce, 2013). Innovators drive change. They tend to be social outliers who do not strongly impact their colleagues (Galloway, 2019). They are generally receptive to unknown things and tend to depend on their values and judgment. The early adopters typically respect innovators; however, most of the faculty might doubt the innovators due to their visionary nature (Rogers, 2003).

2. **Early adopters** represent roughly 13.5 percent of a faculty. They are opinion leaders who are admired and highly regarded by the organization. Like innovators, early adopters readily embrace change early, but they tend to be more cautious than innovators. They are influencers who like to convey ideas and integrate them in beneficial ways. Early adopters are normally respected by the majority of staff (Rogers, 2003). The innovators and early adopters are considered the dreamers and promoters of change (Rogers, 2003).

3. The **early majority** comprises nearly 34 percent of staff. Those in the early majority are deliberate; and although they are rarely leaders, they frequently adapt to change before the average team member. Staff members who are in the early majority look for practical benefits and tend to wait until they see the change succeed in practice (Rogers, 2003).

4. The **late majority**, another 34 percent of the workforce, is similar to the early majority except those in the late majority expect a great deal of help and support before they are willing to commit to change (Pearce, 2013). Members of the late majority can be skeptical. They frequently adopt an innovation or change initiative only after a majority of staff has tried it (Rogers, 2003).

The early majority and late majority (68 percent of the school staff) are the critical mass that ensures the adoption of change (Pearce, 2013).

5. The remaining 16 percent of the staff is known as the **laggards** because they lag behind the other faculty members in accepting and adopting change. They are slow to accept the transformation because they value tradition or are suspicious of new ideas (Rogers, 2003). Many are so resistant to change that they change only when they are forced (Pearce, 2013).

Rogers's (2003) data support DuFour and colleagues' (2016) and Ian Jukes's (2017) assertions that your school will require at least 15 percent of your staff to initiate, embrace, and drive a change in order for the rest of the staff to adopt the change. You will note in figure 1.1, the innovators (2.5 percent) and early adopters (13.5 percent) make up roughly 15 percent of the organization (Rogers, 2003). It is from that 15 percent that your guiding coalition will most likely come. Figure 1.2 compares the range of characteristics of the five types of adopters.

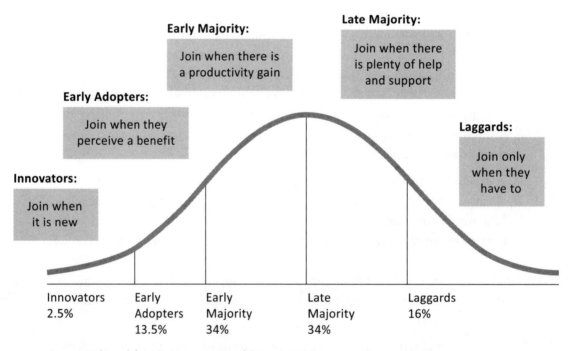

Source: Adapted from Pearce, 2013 and Rogers, 2003.

FIGURE 1.1: Everett M. Rogers's innovation adoption curve.

Adopter Categories				
Innovators	Early Adopters	Early Majority	Late Majority	Laggards
Visionaries and Enthusiasts		Mainstream Adopters		Resisters
• Realize dreams • Drive change • Aren't afraid to fail • Explore in iterations • Have a high tolerance for risk, uncertainty, and ambiguity • Are adventurers • Initiate change • Are internally motivated to change • Are respected by early adopters, but doubted by the masses	• Are evangelists • Embrace change • Have self-efficacy • Like to be first to try, use, engage, or buy something • Try out new ideas in a careful way • Are inspired by what's new • Like integrating new ideas in useful ways • Are influencers—like to convey ideas • Are respected by the majority	• Are pragmatists • Accept change sooner than the late majority • Are deliberate • Adopt what's practical—weigh out pros and cons and think it out • Go along—seldom lead • Help change gain mass appeal • Wait for success in practice	• Are skeptics • Accept change later than the early majority • Adopt after proven success • Often adopt out of necessity, not choice • Go along with peers • Like to know the rules and are creatures of habit • Jump in when "everyone is doing it"	• Are change averse • Value tradition • Do not lead • Are suspicious of new innovations • Often wait until forced to adopt change • Feel threatened or very uncomfortable by uncertainty and change • Do not buy into new ideas

Source: Adapted from Center for Creative Emergence, 2011; James, 2012; Rogers, 2003.

FIGURE 1.2: Characteristics of the five types of change adopters.

Opinion Leaders and Influencers

Use figure 1.3 to identify members of your teaching staff who exhibit the desired characteristics to become members of your guiding coalition. Think about the members of your faculty who exhibit the characteristics in the figure's first two columns, and enter their names in the third column. Keep in mind that some of those you identify might not currently be in formal leadership positions. Base your membership decisions on these characteristics as opposed to position, years of experience, politics, and so on.

In addition to making your list, you might consider asking your current administrative team to review the characteristics and individually complete the tool. Once all members of your current team complete their lists, you can compare the lists of names to see whose names appear most frequently.

Characteristics of Innovators	Characteristics of Early Adopters	Staff Members to Consider
• Realize dreams • Initiate and drive change • Have a high tolerance for risk, uncertainty, and ambiguity • Are not afraid of failure • Have an internal motivation to change • Are respected by the early adopters • Join when the change or idea is new • Are doubted by most of the staff • Love exploration • Imagine the possibilities that change might bring • Relish being on the cutting edge • Bring innovation from outside to inside the organization • Are venturesome	• Embrace change • Like to be first to try, use, and engage new ideas • Try out new ideas with caution • Find inspiration in anything new • Like to find useful ways to implement new ideas • Like to share new ideas • Are respected and held in high regard by the early and late majorities • Join when they see benefits in the change or idea • Are admired by others who feel connected to them • Will give ideas a thumbs-up or thumbs-down • Are viewed by others as power brokers • Help reach a tipping point where the rest of the staff will follow their lead and adopt the change • Are deliberate	

Source: Galloway, 2019; James, 2012; Pearce, 2013; Sahin, 2006.

FIGURE 1.3: Tool for creating a list of potential guiding coalition members.

*Visit **go.SolutionTree.com/PLCbooks** for a free reproducible version of this figure.*

Another method for identifying potential guiding coalition members is to have your administrative team members review the characteristics and then ask them whom they would approach for advice when facing a problem or whom they would confide in when seeking suggestions or opinions. Have your team enter the names in the right column. Collect the lists and write down the names that appear the greatest number of times. The resulting list will likely represent your opinion leaders. Opinion leaders can influence their colleagues positively or negatively, so consider the potential impact when forming your guiding coalition. There may be staff members on your list who have no formal or direct authority. Many informal opinion leaders have no authority or power (Galloway, 2019).

Avoiding Elephant Traps

When assembling your guiding coalition or when considering making changes to guiding coalition membership, include someone who can help keep you and the guiding coalition out of elephant traps. An *elephant trap* is a trap that a competent person can easily avoid (Elephant trap, n.d.). In the context of PLCs, an elephant trap is a situation or condition that could trip up a principal or guiding coalition lacking knowledge about PLC basics and processes. Charging a guiding coalition member with the specific responsibility to look for any unseen trips, tricks, or traps that could derail efforts to build a collaborative culture may be a good insurance policy. Anyone designated to keep your best interests at heart must be knowledgeable of the PLC basics to sense or predict trouble ahead.

Potential elephant traps that your guiding coalition may encounter include the following.

- Attempting to move too quickly (or too slowly) with the implementation of PLC processes
- Skipping essential steps in building a collaborative culture by not:
  » Creating a mission or updating an outdated mission
  » Pushing leadership actions and responsibilities out to all collaborative teams (grade level or department) in a consistent manner
  » Providing reflection, debriefing, and processing time during guiding coalition meetings
  » Recognizing or celebrating team efforts
  » Modeling processes and products that are expected of collaborative teacher teams (for example, creating and enforcing team norms, focusing on student learning, and using data to make informed decisions)
- Lacking oversight, follow-up, or support of the work of collaborative teams

A high-performing guiding coalition with the highest levels of trust most likely will not need an individual to protect the team from elephant traps because all team members will be vigilant and courageous enough to inform the principal even if they have bad news or they have opinions contrary to the principal's position. If your team is not that mature at this time, you might consider selecting such a person and discussing with that person his or her role and responsibilities to ensure he or she understands the purpose of the role. You may have someone on the guiding coalition whose opinions you trust and who can honestly tell it like it is without fear of retaliation. The person whom you designate to keep you from falling into any elephant traps and who will look out for your and the guiding coalition's best interests must be a courageous follower. A courageous follower is someone with the courage to challenge the leader. This characteristic is not meant to be confrontational or undermining (Welcome, 2019); instead, it is a built-in pressure relief valve to protect the principal and the team from situations that could prove disastrous. When the principal sees the courageous follower as a critical friend, the guiding coalition and collaborative teams ultimately benefit. The courageous follower concept is explored in more detail in the "Develop Courageous Followers" section of chapter 6 (page 125).

Application for Guiding Coalition Membership

Figure 1.4 is a sample letter for application for the position of school guiding coalition member. This sample resource can provide principals and guiding coalitions with the means to gather information from applicants to then use to assist them in the guiding coalition application and selection process. This sample application and similar resources can serve as alternative approaches to forming your guiding coalition or can serve as supportive tools to assist with your selection process.

Dear _____,

Background

The fundamental purpose of our school is to continuously increase learning for all students. To accomplish this goal, both teachers and administrators must put forth a collective effort to achieve the following.

- Guide and support the faculty and staff to embrace that all students need to learn at high levels (grade level or higher).
- Learn and then share with faculty and staff research-based best practice that aligns with continuously increasing learning for all students.
- Continuously foster a school culture in which the faculty and staff passionately strive to increase learning for all students by analyzing data.

Eligibility

Our school's guiding coalition will be composed of both administrators and teachers who intrinsically seek to work with other adults on campus so they can continuously increase learning for all students. While all teachers and administrators are welcome to apply, the guiding coalition will include representatives from all academic departments and grade levels. Please note that the principal and a representative from the teachers' association will automatically appear on our school's guiding coalition.

Characteristics

Interested applicants must possess the following characteristics.

- Optimism in our quest to increase learning for all students (In short, a "Yes, we can!" attitude is highly desired.)

- Honesty and the ability to focus in on situations we, as a faculty and staff, can control when seeking to increase learning for all students, versus those challenges (such as poverty, lack of resources at home, and lack of academic foundation for students) we cannot control
- A desire to work with and assist other adults on our campus to reach their fullest potential as professionals

Skills

Interested applicants must be willing to develop the following skills.

- The ability to positively influence other adults on campus to think differently and thus do differently
- The ability to work with others to increase the productivity (learning) of the organization (our school)
- The ability to support faculty and staff members so they embrace and commit to change in policies, practices, and procedures aimed at increasing learning for all students

Interested applicants need apply by _____. Please submit a letter of interest detailing why you seek this position and what qualifications you possess that you feel will contribute to the guiding coalition's overall purpose, as described on this form. Please also include one letter of recommendation from any individual who can attest that you have the leadership skills sought for our school's guiding coalition.

Source: Muhammad & Cruz, 2019, p. 121.

FIGURE 1.4: Sample application for the position of school guiding coalition member.

*Visit **go.SolutionTree.com/PLCbooks** for a free reproducible version of this figure.*

Figure 1.5 (page 26) is a rubric of characteristics required of guiding coalition members to assist principals and guiding coalition members with determining which applicants might be best suited to join the guiding coalition. This resource provides the means to score the characteristics necessary to be an effective team member. Scores will give the team a way to compare all applicants against each other based on common characteristics required for the position.

Conclusion

Regardless of where your school is on the journey to becoming a PLC, you should regularly evaluate your leadership team's ability to lead your school's transformation. If you determine your guiding coalition is cranking on all cylinders, then you are at a green light. Celebrate the fact that you are moving in the right direction—full steam ahead! If there are minor changes that you need to make, you are at a yellow light: proceed with caution. You must build on the positive aspects you already have in place on your team and make changes that will get your team back on track. If your leadership team is nonexistent, focuses on the wrong things, or has you feeling like you are constantly herding cats, you are at a red light. *Stop!* Break out the PLC emergency defibrillator! A major overhaul is required, beginning with analyzing your existing guiding coalition or taking the necessary steps to create a guiding coalition.

Characteristics Required of Guiding Coalition Members	3 Beyond Proficient	2 Proficient	1 Below Proficient	Applicant Rating (Circle one.)
Continuously learns	The applicant is seen as a leader in terms of improving their practice. They are constantly seeking out new and better methods to ensure high levels of learning for all, including academic, behavioral, social, and emotional learning for students. They see the benefit of growing their leadership abilities so that their influence exceeds their reach.	The applicant has improved their practice over time. They often wait for others to inform them of a new resource or method. They typically do not share new practices and their results without being prompted. The applicant occasionally demonstrates leadership but with an emphasis that is not always student centered. They may have a desire or natural ability but not both.	The applicant does not seek out new methods of doing things. They tend to do things because they have always done them that way. They see leadership in the guiding coalition as advocating for the needs of the adults on their team.	3 2 1
Is student centered	Everything the applicant does is in the best interest of students. The applicant uses a common-sense approach to academic and behavioral instruction, classroom policies and procedures, and the application of schoolwide practices to ensure high levels of learning for all.	The applicant usually focuses on what is best for students. There are some examples of their relying too heavily on established practices and history to dictate what should be done next. They do make accommodations for some or most students when it comes to academic and behavioral learning.	The applicant demonstrates little flexibility in terms of applying practices and procedures in their classroom and the school. The rule is the rule, and they typically don't make exceptions. They tend to teach one way and change very little to help students learn and grow.	3 2 1
Is positive	The applicant is a continuous source of positivity. They are seen as someone who sees the good in every single situation, and they rarely waver when there is a difficult issue to solve. People believe they can do anything when working with this individual.	The applicant is usually upbeat. They can demonstrate some negativity occasionally. When working with others, the applicant sometimes allows for negativity to present itself.	The applicant frequently sends a message of negativity. They often are heard making excuses for why something won't work. They may say they are positive, but they do not always demonstrate it.	3 2 1

	3	2	1
Stays focused	The applicant has a laser-like focus on student achievement. They "look in the mirror" as opposed to "look out the window" when it comes to student achievement. They never blame variables over which they have no control.	The applicant focuses on students and their needs most of the time. They occasionally make mention of or blame factors such as a student's family situation, socioeconomic factors, or effort. Overall, however, they do what they can to ensure learning for all.	The applicant may say that they are focused on what they can do to help students, but they frequently fall back on blaming variables outside their control. They refer to the idea that they have done everything they can and call into question students' desire to comply.
Has influence	The applicant has developed trust with others through deep, meaningful relationships that are based on mutual respect and commitment to our mission. People listen intently when the applicant speaks and seek out the applicant's opinions, thoughts, and ideas. The applicant puts a great emphasis on cultural work within the staff or their team.	The applicant is seen as a contributing member of the staff, their team, or their grade level. They frequently go along with the group and don't question the reason for a decision. They tend to excel at structural tasks versus cultural work and consensus building.	The applicant is not a person in the building whom others would follow. They either haven't built trusting relationships with others based on our mission or haven't been here long enough to do so.
Drives improvement	The applicant drives improvement in our building. They are not afraid to challenge the staff appropriately. They constructively handle dissent from teammates or staff and use dissenting voices to learn, grow, and acknowledge their errors.	The applicant suggests methods of improvement, but there may not be any follow-through on the application of the suggestions. The applicant demonstrates a desire to have the group or team evolve, but the process is clunky and the outcomes are inconsistent.	The applicant has not challenged staff to change or grow to ensure learning for all. They worry about whether other staff or team members will like or respect them. They may not recognize that growth is necessary.
Total Applicant Rating			

Source: © 2020 by Jed Kees.

FIGURE 1.5: Sample guiding coalition applicant rubric.

Visit go.SolutionTree.com/PLCbooks for a free reproducible version of this figure.

Chapter 2, "Leading the PLC Basics," will help you determine if the basic PLC concepts are at the center of your school's transformation. When these concepts and processes become the main thing, it becomes easier to stay on the correct path to becoming a learning-focused organization.

In the following pages, you will find next-step, FAQ, and reflection sections to help you in your work to create a powerful guiding coalition.

▶ Next Steps ▶

Consider the current status of your guiding coalition. Have your current leadership team or guiding coalition complete figure 1.6 to determine which effective practices your school currently has in place. Use this readiness tool to determine if your guiding coalition or leadership team is set up for success or if improvement is needed.

Effective PLC Practices	Not Initiated	Initiated but Not Completed (In Progress)	Completed
All certificated personnel are on meaningful collaborative teams.			
All administrators are on a team (for example, the guiding coalition or a different collaborative team).			
All teams have a representative on the guiding coalition. All personnel are represented on the guiding coalition.			
The guiding coalition has team-developed, team-approved norms that are referred to and used during every meeting.			
Guiding coalition meetings are scheduled to take place once a week.			
The guiding coalition develops and uses an agenda to guide every meeting.			
The guiding coalition agenda exclusively focuses time and efforts on PLC topics.			
Consensus is the preferred decision-making option.			

The guiding coalition is structured like a collaborative teacher team and operates like a collaborative teacher team. It models the expected behaviors and actions of a collaborative team. It generates products similar to those required of collaborative teacher teams.

FIGURE 1.6: Effective practices for the guiding coalition and collaborative teams.

*Visit **go.SolutionTree.com/PLCbooks** for a free reproducible version of this figure.*

Have your leadership team or guiding coalition members share and discuss their responses. Is everything in place for them to take on the roles and responsibilities required to lead your PLC, or are there practices that need attention? Have your team complete the following worksheet (figure 1.7, page 30) to determine your guiding coalition's readiness and to plan how to address any practices that need attention.

 FAQs

How many members should the guiding coalition have?

Although there is no set number for teams, most guiding coalitions have one teacher from each grade level or department plus a representative from activity teachers, special education teachers, counselors, and other specialized teams as appropriate. The authors of *Learning by Doing* note that roughly 15 percent of faculties are opinion leaders (DuFour et al., 2016). Opinion leaders are so respected and trusted that they can influence the rest of their school's faculty (DuFour et al., 2016).

In his blog, *Learn What's Going On!*, Ian Jukes (2017), cofounder and executive director of Infosavvy21, shares his observation of a large school of sardines while he was visiting the Monterey Bay Aquarium in Monterey, California. He notes that the enormous mass of sardines was swimming in one direction. Suddenly, in the blink of an eye, the entire school would turn 180 degrees. Realizing the sardines could not possibly be using extrasensory perception, Twitter, Snapchat, or Facebook to cause such a large school to turn all at once, he studied the large mass to see what could be causing the change. He observed very closely that a small group of sardines within the larger school would begin turning in a different direction. To Jukes (2017), it appeared that this small group of sardines caused "conflict, discomfort, and distress" among the others in the school! He noticed that when a critical mass of what he called "the committed sardines" made the turn, "the rest of the school instantly turned and followed" (Jukes, 2017). In his blog post, he defines the committed sardines as those who truly believed in the change. The committed sardines did not make up 50 percent or 60 percent, or more, of the school (Jukes, 2017). The committed sardines were only about 10 percent to 15 percent of the school, the same percentage that DuFour and colleagues (2016) note. PLC leaders may find the task of creating a guiding coalition easier using these

Where Do We Go From Here? Worksheet
Guiding Coalition Readiness

Effective PLC Practices	What steps or activities must the guiding coalition initiate to implement this practice?	Who will be responsible for initiating or sustaining these steps or activities?	What is a realistic timeline for embedding the practice into the guiding coalition's routine or structure?	What will the guiding coalition use to assess the effectiveness of its actions?
All certificated personnel are on meaningful teams.				
All administrators are on a team.				
All teams and all personnel are represented on the guiding coalition.				
The guiding coalition has team-developed, team-approved norms that are referred to and used during every meeting.				

Guiding coalition meetings are scheduled to take place once a week.

The guiding coalition develops and uses an agenda to guide every meeting.

The guiding coalition agenda exclusively focuses time and efforts on PLC topics.

Consensus is the preferred decision-making option.

The guiding coalition is structured like a collaborative teacher team and operates like a collaborative teacher team. It models what is expected of collaborative teacher teams.

Source: Adapted from DuFour et al., 2016.

FIGURE 1.7: Where Do We Go From Here? worksheet.

Visit go.SolutionTree.com/PLCbooks for a free reproducible version of this figure.

suggested percentages as a guide. There is no specific rule or number to use when creating the team; however, using the general guideline of 10 to 15 percent of total staff might serve as a good target.

How often and for how long should the guiding coalition meet?

The optimum schedule is to meet once a week for at least one hour during the initial phases of your development as a professional learning community. If your school schedule will not allow your guiding coalition to meet weekly, meeting every other week for one hour will suffice; however, this will affect time for and depth of implementation. When guiding coalitions attempt to meet less than every other week, leadership processes will be seriously impaired. Teams that meet once a month for forty-five minutes to an hour spend the time reviewing work and decisions from the previous meeting and are not left any time to move forward.

What are the different roles of the guiding coalition members?

Roles among guiding coalition members would be the same as with all collaborative teams. Typical roles might include:

- Facilitator—Leads the team toward accomplishing its tasks and goals, participates in discussions and the decision-making process, and focuses on meeting content and leading processes

- Recorder—Keeps notes and creates a team memory of each session

- Timekeeper—Keeps the team meetings on schedule according to the agenda

- Process observer—Observes the processes used during each meeting and shares pluses (successes) and deltas (suggested changes) with the team (Process observers are not sergeants at arms; the entire team is responsible for enforcing the team's norms and accountability protocol.)

- Reporter—Functions either internally or externally to the team; reports out any communication written by the recorder

- Participants—Work together to process information and share opinions in a safe, confidential environment; support and advise the principal on the work required for the success of the PLC

Currently, I have a leadership team composed of my assistant principal, one dean, one guidance counselor, the head of our exceptional (special) education department, and one instructional coach. Our exceptional education department head is the only classroom teacher on the team. Our team leads all aspects of the school, from addressing discipline issues to implementing our school-improvement plan, to managing the facilities, to enforcing board policies. We do it all. Which might be a better decision—add classroom teachers to our existing team and add the PLC leadership responsibilities to our plates, or create a separate guiding coalition with teacher representatives from each team who will specifically lead the PLC process?

In a perfect world, the best answer would be to create a separate guiding coalition made of teacher leaders who represent all teachers on staff. This team would exclusively focus on leading your PLC process. The agendas would focus on every aspect of PLC leadership. The team would have no distractions from other issues.

If, for some reason, you are unable to create a separate guiding coalition to lead your PLC efforts, the next best choice would be to include representatives from each grade level or content area to expand the membership of your current team that represents every teacher on staff. Current circumstances and conditions would determine which path to take. For example, if you do not have available qualified, interested personnel to serve on a separate guiding coalition, you may be left with the only option of adding to your current leadership team. If you do have enough qualified, interested personnel available to create a separate PLC-focused guiding coalition, but they are currently overloaded with conflicting obligations and responsibilities, you may wish to re-evaluate how many teams you have, who is serving on multiple teams, and who is not serving in any capacity. The purpose to looking at how your teams are currently organized is to assess levels of responsibility and commitment in order to determine where shifts in assignments might be made.

Another helpful tip is to look at what responsibilities your current leadership team has. If they are overloaded with "all aspects of the school, from addressing discipline issues to implementing our school-improvement plan, to managing the facilities, to enforcing board policies," perhaps you can reduce the number of responsibilities and redistribute them to other staff members.

A challenge I face is how to find a balance between keeping my best leaders on the guiding coalition and giving those with leadership potential time to serve. How do I resolve this issue?

You will want to address or review this challenge every year. You certainly do not want to run your thoroughbreds into the ground by keeping them on the guiding coalition indefinitely. Nor do you want to have frequent turnover that could cause you to start anew annually. A possible solution might be found in the middle, where a third of the positions on the guiding coalition rotate each year to bring in new blood, new ideas, and new perspectives from your budding leadership. Through some type of rotation, you will concurrently have seasoned leaders, personnel with some leadership experience, and new leaders on your team.

Of course, posing the challenge to your guiding coalition might prove helpful as you make the decision. The team's opinions and perspectives will prove invaluable. You may find yourself trying several approaches until the most effective and efficient solution reveals itself to you and your team. There is no right way to assemble your guiding coalition. Ideas that seem to work for one school may not work for another. Revisiting the makeup of the team annually could help fine-tune your selection process.

When I became the principal of my school, I inherited an established leadership team that was in shambles. What should I do?

You might consider a few options based on your experience, your leadership style, and your school's needs. Option one would be to hit the restart button. After observing the team for a while, you may decide the team is not salvageable. You may not have the resources to get the team on track. Thank the current team members for their service, honor their work, and recognize them during a staff meeting. Start afresh building your new team. By naming it a *guiding coalition* and giving it a new purpose and direction to move your school to become a PLC, you might take away the sting that former members feel when you disband the team. Meet with members, preferably individually, and explain your new direction. Also, explain that they may become part of the new team or perhaps their leadership experiences might be required in another area. Let them down easily. Monitor the more disgruntled former team members to ensure their actions do not become a personnel matter. Check in with them occasionally to let them know you care and you are interested in their well-being.

Option two would be to meet with the team, refocus the team members on their purpose, and build shared knowledge of the PLC concepts and processes. The team may become more effective under your guidance and leadership. Be patient and give the team time to respond.

A third option might be to drop some team members and bring on new members based on the needs, strengths, and liabilities of the current team. Give the former team members the reason for your changes, and consider finding other leadership opportunities in the school where their talents might fit best.

Reflection

Think about the leadership structure and processes currently in place in your school. Answer questions 1–3, and then fill out the "Action Plan for Making Structural Changes to Your Guiding Coalition" as you answer questions 4–6. This reproducible will help you plan for necessary structural change to your guiding coalition.

1. Is there seamless alignment between how your leadership team operates and how your collaborative learning teams function, or is there a disconnect between the two? What evidence do you have that leads you to this answer?

2. Does your guiding coalition experience and model collaborative processes for the teacher teams it leads, or does it more or less direct those teams to be collaborative? What evidence do you have?

3. Do you believe that more traditional, top-down leaders will find it difficult to lead a collaborative, team-focused culture?

4. After reading chapter 1, what one change might you make in your current leadership structure that will help your guiding coalition become a more collaborative team?

5. What actions will you and your team need to take to facilitate that change?

6. What evidence will you look for to determine if your change made the impact you planned?

Action Plan for Making Structural Changes to Your Guiding Coalition

Leadership Structural Change That Will Make Your Guiding Coalition More Collaborative	Actions You Will Take	Evidence of Impact

CHAPTER 2

LEADING THE PLC BASICS

The leader sees things through the eyes of his followers. He puts himself in their shoes and helps them make their dreams come true. The leader does not say, "Get going!" Instead, he says, "Let's go!" and leads the way.

—Wilferd Peterson

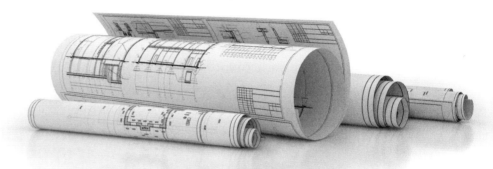

School change does not just happen naturally. For your school to become a PLC or improve as a PLC, much more must happen than the passage of time. You must *lead* the process. If you do not understand what a PLC looks like at every level, you will have an extremely difficult time moving your school in the proper direction.

School leaders must first commit to the process of change; in poker terms, they must go "all in" on the idea of creating a school where teachers work collaboratively for the benefit of all students. When personal commitment is weak or absent, the change process can easily wander off track. It can be very disruptive when leadership is lukewarm and wavers. Indecisiveness and hesitation can breed confusion and division among staff.

A commitment to creating a collaborative culture is one of the big ideas of a PLC (DuFour et al., 2016). Once you as a leader understand the process of moving your school forward and commit to leading that process by whatever it takes, you are ready to share the process and its *why* with your guiding coalition. Effective leaders implement and lead the change process through the distribution of commitment. By dispersing your commitment to becoming a PLC to your guiding coalition, you are creating the essential nucleus of leadership charged with the responsibility to move your school in a new direction.

Creating a Collaborative Culture

To create a collaborative culture, you must first assess whether your school is ready for collaborative work. Compared to PLCs, more traditional schools are likely to have larger numbers of individual teachers who work in isolation. These teachers tend to have no real connection to or accountability with others. They might see themselves as self-employed workers or private contractors. They come to school, do their thing, and go home. They teach the material, and if students get it, that's great! There is a lot of material in the book to cover, so teachers have to give students the opportunity to learn and then move on.

If teachers in traditional schools are not private contractors, they might gather into loosely formed groups. They find themselves working in grade-level or department-level silos with no contact with other teams. These loosely created groupings of teachers whose only connection is a grade level or content area are not collaborative teams. There is much more to teamwork than being connected by name or subject area.

Collaborative learning teams in a PLC must have the following three elements or criteria in place to operate as a team: (1) a common goal, (2) interdependence, and (3) mutual accountability (DuFour et al., 2016). Remove any one of the three elements, and teams fall back into *groups*. The only way groups can become teams is to change how the individuals within them work together.

A Common Goal

First, teams have a *common goal*—a single focus for their work. Whether a team of two or a team of forty-two, all teams require a common goal that all members clearly understand, agree on, commit to, and work toward. Working toward a common goal gives collaborative teams many opportunities to communicate in common, team-focused terms.

Interdependence

Second, members of collaborative teams in a PLC work together *interdependently*: "You depend on me; I depend on you." Interdependence occurs when everyone brings something to the table, not when one individual does most of the work or preparation and the rest of the group shares the credit.

In highly collaborative cultures, interdependence can lead to synergy. *Synergy* is "the interaction or cooperation of two or more organizations, substances, or other agents to produce a combined effect greater than the sum of their separate effects" (Synergy, n.d.). A mathematical formula for synergy might look like this: $1 + 1 = 3$ (Burgin & Meissner, 2017). As your guiding coalition's leader, your personal goal for your team is to reach synergy in the major decisions you make.

Educator and author Stephen Covey (1989) describes synergy as coming up with a third alternative. Decision making is not about following your ideas just because you are the principal, nor is it about going with the ideas of your coalition or individual team members. It's about finding a better way. The third alternative is reached when you and your guiding coalition arrive at a solution, a decision, or an idea that neither you nor your team would have arrived at individually (Covey, 1989).

In *The Seven Habits of Highly Effective People*, Covey (1989) suggests a four-step process for finding synergistic solutions (Eaton, 2011).

1. Ask the people involved if they are willing to go for a solution that is better than what either side has come up with before.

2. Define *success*. Describe a clear vision of the job to be done, create a list of criteria for success that would make everyone happy, and develop criteria that would move the team beyond members' entrenched demands.

3. Brainstorm and search for new solutions. Turn your thinking upside down and experiment with radical possibilities.

4. Keep working at it until you reach synergy. You can tell when that happens because there is a "burst of creative dynamism and excitement in the room. At that point, hesitation and conflict are gone." (p. 22)

Third-alternative solutions are reached through this out-of-the-box thinking. Ideas for these creative solutions do not come from two opposing views; they are conceived when competing interests give up their closely held ideas and opinions for the benefit of the organization. Grounding the problem-solving process in the organization's foundational beliefs moves the discussion from what benefits the individual to what is best for the organization as a whole.

Mutual Accountability

The third element of a team in a PLC is that all team members are *mutually accountable*. They are mutually accountable for their behavior as a team, for addressing violations of team norms, for the results of their work, and for the products they develop. Members of collaborative teams hold each other accountable for how they act, for how they meet team expectations, and for how effectively they work together. Collaborative team members monitor their accountability to each other internally; they do not wait to get so far off track that an administrator has to step in. They do not wait to be told how to proceed.

High-performing collaborative teams operate on a foundation of honesty and trust. When team protocols are broken, the team is responsible for confronting and addressing the violations by using measures the team established at its inception. Pre-established protocols help teams focus on behaviors and not on personalities.

Figure 2.1 (page 40) is a tool to assess the current status of your guiding coalition. In each row, select which of the two descriptors best describes your guiding coalition. For each row in which you circle *group*, create an action plan so your group will work more as a team. Collaborative teacher teams can also use this resource in the same way. Team members can complete the tool individually and then discuss their responses with the entire team to determine whether they must take action to move from being a group to being a team.

Group Descriptor	Team Descriptor	Group or Team Status (Circle *team* if your team meets the team descriptor. Circle *group* if the group descriptor is more accurate.)	Required Action (If you circled *group*, write down what action is required to move your group to a team.)
Group sessions include information sharing and perspective sharing.	Team sessions include discussion, decision making, problem solving, and planning.	Group Team	
The group's purpose, goals, and approaches to work are shaped by the group leader.	The team's purpose, goals, and approaches to work are shaped by the team leader with the team members.	Group Team	
The group leader has more responsibility and authority than all other group members.	The team leader has equal responsibility and authority to all other team members.	Group Team	
Collaboration is not guaranteed. A few group members may do the majority of the work.	Team members collaborate and divide the work to achieve the team's goals.	Group Team	
The group has one leader.	The team depends on shared leadership among its members.	Group Team	
Group members create individual products.	The team creates collective work products.	Group Team	
The group discusses, decides, and delegates the work.	The team discusses, decides, and does the work together.	Group Team	
Group members have individual accountability.	The team depends on mutual accountability.	Group Team	

| Roles and responsibilities are not generally assigned to individuals. | Roles and responsibilities are assigned to each team member. | Group

Team | |
| Group members tend to work independently. | Team members work interdependently. | Group

Team | |

Source: Hasa, 2016; Jose, 2014; Naywinaung, 2014; O'Leary, 2016; Ribeiro, 2020.

FIGURE 2.1: Tool for determining whether your guiding coalition is a group, a team, or somewhere in between.

*Visit **go.SolutionTree.com/PLCbooks** for a free reproducible version of this figure.*

Leading the Three Big Ideas of a PLC

A PLC has three big ideas on which all members—from the school leader to the guiding coalition to the collaborative teacher teams—focus. These three big ideas are (DuFour et al., 2016):

1. A focus on student learning

2. A collaborative culture and collective responsibility

3. A results orientation

At the beginning of your transition to a PLC, guiding coalition members may struggle to consistently keep these big ideas at the forefront of their team discussions. Therefore, it is incumbent on you, as leader, to frequently bring these ideas to a conscious level. Your guiding coalition will follow your lead and will eventually lead their teams similarly (DuFour et al., 2021).

Leading the Focus on Learning

The members of your guiding coalition must ensure that the collaborative teams they lead focus on the right work. One simple yet excellent way to lead your school's focus on student learning is to make the topic part of a formal team discussion. Ask your guiding coalition members, "Give a recent example of a time when your collaborative team specifically discussed student learning. Did your discussion get off track and another topic creep in? How did you redirect the focus of the conversation back to learning?" If your guiding coalition is new to the PLC process, you might reframe your questions to, "What are typical topics of discussion when your grade-level or department teams meet? If during our protected collaborative team time our discussions are to be focused on student learning, what can we do to move from off-topic talk to talk focused on student learning?" An open discussion on this big idea has several benefits. As principal, you are modeling what the conversation should sound like and what the process of focusing squarely on the topic looks like for the guiding coalition. You are bringing student learning front and center for all to see and hear. You are telling your team, "Student learning is *job one* in our school, and everything we do must support it!" When team members share how they are focusing on student learning and what they do when the focus gets fuzzy, they learn from each other about how to lead student learning and how to manage barriers. Sharing collective best practices is a hallmark of high-performing collaborative teams.

Voices From the Field

Failure to establish a guiding coalition focused on increasing evidence of learning for all students or failure to provide members with the knowledge of how to do so and the skill to support and hold teams accountable is equivalent to not having the necessary motor in a race car to effectively compete in the Indy 500! Establishing a healthy and functional guiding coalition is critically important if we are going to build a culture focused on learning for all.

—High School Principal, California

Leading the Collaborative Culture and Collective Responsibility

The second big idea is building a collaborative culture and collective responsibility. Note that the focus is not solely on collaboration. The distinction between *collaboration* and a *collaborative culture* is significant. Collaboration does not always create a collaborative culture. Collaboration can lead to developing a collaborative culture; however, focusing exclusively on collaboration might lead to only short-term benefits. There may be some feel-good results from collaborating. For example, team members may feel they are getting along better, communicating better, or reaching agreement more often; however, the enculturation of collaborative processes demands much more than just getting along. Teams might begin the process of working together, but if that work is not substantially sustained and firmly and deeply embedded into the school's culture, it will most likely fade over time. Collaboration by itself is not enough.

A big question for your guiding coalition is, "Are your teams collaborating, or are they contributing to building a collaborative culture?" Based on their answers and the discussion that follows, guiding coalition members will determine what work they must do. Leaders must discuss how the guiding coalition can lead pockets of collaboration mixed with pockets of lukewarm collaborative practices and non-collaborative work or toxic teams toward becoming a collaborative culture.

For your school to become a collaborative culture, all your teams have the responsibility to work collaboratively. Should two or three teams not meet the definition of being collaborative, the remaining teams have a collective responsibility to provide support and assistance to help the team leaders and teams that are struggling. The team leaders who are in need of support and assistance also are collectively responsible to the guiding coalition and to their collaborative teams to be open to accepting help and doing whatever it takes to develop a more collaborative team.

Ultimately, it is the guiding coalition's responsibility to ensure that all teams are functioning collaboratively and assist when they are not. One way to assess if teams are working together collaboratively is to complete figure 2.1 (page 40), the same tool for determining whether your guiding coalition is a group, a team, or somewhere in between.

Leading the Focus on Results

The third big idea is a focus on results. Big idea 3 links idea 1 (student learning) and idea 2 (collaborative culture and collective responsibility). Unless your teams regularly use data, information, and results to determine their strategies, actions, and responses, they will be flying blindly. Without data, collaborative cultures will struggle to improve student learning. Results inform teams which students are learning, which students are struggling, and which students need what levels of intervention or enrichment. Results also inform collaborative teams of strengths and weaknesses in their teaching practices and strategies.

To effectively focus on results, the guiding coalition may ask questions such as, "Are our teams centering their collaborative team discussions and concentrating their work around the four critical questions?" and "What can we do to ensure that all teams are collaboratively creating and giving common formative assessments and using the results to drive their instruction and to provide intervention, enrichment, and extension?" (The critical questions can be found on page 44 in the section titled "Leading the Four Critical Questions of a PLC.")

Leading Fidelity With PLC Principles and Concepts

PLCs offer the promise of providing schools with the opportunities and optimism for improved student learning if schools adhere to PLC concepts with fidelity. Fidelity is key. Spotty, infrequent, or poorly done assessments of where your school is, where you are headed, and what leadership actions you need can quickly derail any efforts your school may make in gaining traction. It is the guiding coalition's collective responsibility to ensure that collaborative teacher teams are staying true to the basic PLC concepts. How does your guiding coalition do this? Through frequent monitoring of implementation. For example, when your guiding coalition is ready to introduce team norms and accountability protocols to the entire staff, it discusses the process to roll them out. The guiding coalition reflects on its own experience when it created its norms and protocols. What went well? What needed correction? What did the members learn from the process that will make creating and embedding norms easier and more worthwhile for the teams they serve? How will the guiding coalition introduce norms to the school teams? What professional learning must the guiding coalition provide to the faculty to ensure successful completion and implementation of those norms? How will your guiding coalition monitor the progress of norm development and provide assistance, support, and resources for teams that struggle?

When leading the norm creation process schoolwide, your guiding coalition would not demand that teams "get their norms done" without giving the why, the purpose, or the method. That process spells disaster. Instead, you and your guiding coalition should learn about norms, their purpose, the need for them, and the process to create them. Once the team has a better idea of what norms are and why they are critical to your school's success, it then would create its own norms and accountability protocols to be used during every meeting thereafter. Creating this set of norms accomplishes two outcomes. The first outcome is the guiding coalition members go through the actual process their collaborative teams will later use to create their team norms. The second outcome is your guiding coalition has a useful set of norms it will use to meet its needs throughout the school year.

Following the creation of its norms, your guiding coalition is ready to roll out the norm creation process to all teams. After experiencing the development of its own norms, your team members are ready and equipped to go back to their grade-level or department teams and duplicate the process that led them to create a quality set of norms for the guiding coalition. Once each team's norms and accountability protocols are complete, the teams submit them to the guiding coalition for review and approval. This way, the guiding coalition can ensure that the teams maintained fidelity to the process, that the norms and protocols are clearly written, and that the norms are appropriate and supportable by the principal (with input from the guiding coalition) once they are put into place.

In their article "Professional Learning Communities Focusing on Results and Data-Use to Improve Student Learning," Marco A. Muñoz and Karen E. Branham (2016) argue that this "implementation fidelity" is critically important to the creation and sustainability of the PLC process. Fidelity cannot be assumed. It is to be frequently assessed. The practice of regularly assessing fidelity to the three big ideas and other vital PLC building blocks can help keep schools from straying too far off the proper path toward improved results for all students (Muñoz & Branham, 2016).

Are your teams staying true to the process that leads schools to become PLCs? Figure 2.2 is an implementation fidelity assessment tool to help your guiding coalition determine where collaborative teams are staying true to the three big ideas and where they need to strengthen fidelity to those big ideas.

While the three big ideas are foundational to a PLC, the four critical questions create the cycle of the work of collaborative teams in a PLC (DuFour et al., 2016).

Leading the Four Critical Questions of a PLC

When collaborative teams ask, "What are we supposed to do during our collaborative team time?" the response should always be, "Your team is to primarily focus on answering the four critical questions of learning." These questions (DuFour et al., 2016) are:

A Focus on Learning			
PLC Concepts That Focus on Learning	Fidelity to Concept Lacking	Partial Fidelity to Concept Evident	Full Fidelity to Concept Evident
Is there fidelity among team members to build shared knowledge about what students must know and be able to do?			
Is there fidelity among team members to clarify criteria for judging the quality of student work and to practice applying those criteria consistently?			
Is there fidelity among team members to monitor student learning through frequent, team-developed common formative assessments?			
Is there fidelity among team members to use a system of interventions guaranteeing that all students receive the necessary support and time to be successful?			
Is there fidelity among team members to provide extension and enrichment once students have mastered skills that are considered to be essential?			
A Collaborative Culture and Collective Responsibility			
PLC Concepts That Focus on a Collaborative Culture and Collective Responsibility	Fidelity to Concept Lacking	Partial Fidelity to Concept Evident	Full Fidelity to Concept Evident
Is there fidelity among team members to organize into collaborative teams?			
Is there fidelity among team members to meet during the workday?			
Is there fidelity among team members to process the critical questions required of collaborative teams?			

FIGURE 2.2: Implementation fidelity assessment tool.

continued →

	Fidelity to Concept Lacking	Partial Fidelity to Concept Evident	Full Fidelity to Concept Evident
Is there fidelity among team members to develop, adhere to, and enforce team norms?			
Is there fidelity among team members to create and submit products as required?			

A Focus on Results			
PLC Concepts That Focus on Results	Fidelity to Concept Lacking	Partial Fidelity to Concept Evident	Full Fidelity to Concept Evident
Is there fidelity among team members to identify and create a strategic and specific, measurable, attainable, results-oriented, and time-bound (SMART) goal for their team?			
Is there fidelity among team members to provide frequent and timely feedback on the performance of their students?			
Is there fidelity among team members to use common formative assessment results to identify students who need additional time and support?			
Is there fidelity among team members to use common formative assessment results to identify strengths and weaknesses in their teaching practices and strategies?			
Is there fidelity among team members to use common formative assessment results to gauge the team's progress toward its SMART goal?			

Source: Adapted from DuFour & DuFour, 2006, and DuFour et al., 2016.

1. What knowledge, skills, and dispositions should every student acquire as a result of this unit, this course, or this grade level?

2. How will we know when each student has acquired the essential knowledge and skills?

3. How will we respond when some students do not learn?

4. How will we extend the learning for students who are already proficient? (p. 36)

During specifically scheduled collaborative team time, answering the four critical questions is the focus of conversation, discussion, and work; it is the only focus. To ensure your grade-level or department-level teams focus on those essential questions, the members of your guiding coalition will want to explore their understanding and experiences in working through the questions themselves before leading their teams through the process.

As the guiding coalition members think through the four critical questions and how they might best guide collaborative teams, they may wish to rework each question to focus on what they (the guiding coalition members) need to know about the collaborative teams. For example, the guiding coalition might reword critical question 1 as, "What do we want our collaborative teams to learn or do as we begin the process of becoming a PLC?" Just as teacher teams will need to determine essential standards when answering question 1 for their students, the guiding coalition's members determine the "essential standards" they want to address with their collaborative teams. Have them go through the process of addressing each question in order, and then debrief the process to discuss the challenges they encountered and strategies for overcoming them. They may want to brainstorm ideas regarding the staff's learning needs using the process tool in figure 2.3.

Step 1: Brainwriting

Have all members of the team brainwrite responses to the question or problem. Brainwriting requires team members to silently reflect and think about their personal thoughts, ideas, suggestions, and so on and write them on a piece of paper. There is no discussion or sharing during this part of the process.

Step 2: Brainstorming

Assign two recorders to stand at blank chart papers at the front of the room. Each recorder should have two wide-tipped markers of different colors (no yellow, pink, red, or light colors). When directed by the team facilitator, all members of the team (including the recorders and facilitator) individually call out their responses. One recorder prints the first response on his or her chart paper. The other recorder records the second response. They alternate writing responses until all responses are recorded. Responses are written in alternating colors to distinguish the entries from each other. Entries should have spaces between them to further distinguish them from each other. There is to be no discussion, no clarification, and no comments or questions during the recording process. There cannot be any interruption that could break the free flow of responses and ideas. Duplicate responses are recorded, and duplicates will be eliminated later. The key to successful brainstorming lies in how well the facilitator leads the process.

FIGURE 2.3: Effective brainstorming process tool for collaborative teams.   continued →

Step 3: Generating New Ideas or Suggestions Based on Responses

During the recording process, participants may think of other ideas and suggestions based on what they see and hear during the brainstorming process. Those new suggestions should be called out as well. If there are limited responses, the team appears stuck, or the brainstorming process slows down, the facilitator might want to ask, "What are you or your colleagues feeling? What might you or your colleagues be hearing? What might you or your colleagues be seeing? What might you or your colleagues be experiencing?" Once all ideas have been recorded, the facilitator should ask the team to silently review the recorded lists to see if there are any more ideas to suggest. The facilitator finally asks the team members to signal agreement that all ideas and suggestions are out and recorded. (Note: Team members are signaling that all ideas are listed. They are not signaling they agree to all the ideas and suggestions.)

Step 4: Clarifying

Looking at the lists, team members are then given the opportunity to ask clarifying questions about terminology, intent, meaning, and so on. When clarification is being sought, the person who offered the idea or response is the person to clarify the response.

Step 5: Eliminating Duplicates

Once clarification is complete, the team will eliminate duplicate responses. The facilitator must ensure the person who suggested a response in question agrees that what he or she suggested is indeed similar to another idea before it is eliminated. The facilitator must not assume ideas are similar just because the wording is similar.

Step 6: Presenting the Final List of Brainstormed Items

Once steps for clarification and elimination of duplicates are complete, your team will have a list of ideas, suggestions, or possible solutions to consider during the decision-making process to follow.

The guiding coalition might come up with essential standards such as the following.

- Collaborative teams must know what a PLC is.

- Collaborative teams must know the characteristics of a PLC.

- Collaborative teams must know how those characteristics are related to the research on effective teaching practices.

- Collaborative teams must know the benefits to working in collaborative teams.

The guiding coalition may also decide it is critical to introduce PLC terms and definitions to the staff so that a common vocabulary can be developed and understood during collaborative team time (Keating et al., 2008).

Once it has a list of essential standards for its teams, the guiding coalition then prioritizes them to determine which ones are to be met first. Those become the guiding coalition's answer to the question, "What do we want our teachers to learn?"

The next step is to address critical question 2, which the guiding coalition may ask in this way: "How will we know if our collaborative teams learned and understand the concepts and characteristics of a PLC?" Just as teacher teams begin with the end in mind, the guiding coalition will need to develop a way to assess how the collaborative teams accomplished what was required of them in question 1. In other words, the guiding coalition members will create a common formative assessment *before* presenting the essential standards they have chosen for their teams so they have a way to determine whether the essential standards have been met.

When creating the common formative assessment, the guiding coalition discusses and agrees on its "look-fors" and "listen-fors" to determine if grade-level or department-level teams know and understand the concepts behind collaboration. Figure 2.4 (page 50) provides your guiding coalition with a set of look-fors and listen-fors to assess whether your collaborative teams are conducting their team meetings properly, according to PLC processes and products. This observation and feedback tool serves as a guide for reviewing and refining the collaborative team processes and is not meant to be used as an evaluative instrument or to be used during the performance-appraisal process. Responses to the feedback topics at the bottom of the tool can provide teams with opportunities for reflection, improvement, and professional growth.

Members of the guiding coalition should meet with their collaborative teams a few times to introduce the PLC concepts and administer the common formative assessment. They then bring their observations back to the guiding coalition meetings to debrief, discuss, and determine the next steps. They examine the results of their common formative assessment to answer revised versions of question 3 ("What do we do for collaborative teams that don't understand?") and question 4 ("What do we do for collaborative teams that understand the concepts and characteristics of a PLC?").

Guiding coalition members may ask, "What do the staff understand? What do they not understand? What is confusing them? What do faculty members seem to support? Are there any misunderstandings or pockets of resistance?" Their comments and observations will lead them to identify what they need to celebrate; what they need to support, clarify, or share differently; and what they can do as a next step for extending their teams' learning.

Once the guiding coalition becomes familiar with the experience of addressing the four critical questions, the members will find it easier to lead their teams through the process of identifying essential standards, creating common formative assessments to determine whether students learned the standards, and coming up with plans for intervention and extension.

Conclusion

Your guiding coalition is charged with leading the PLC process by first learning and experiencing what will be required of each collaborative team. Once the school's leadership has a clear understanding of the why, the what, the how, the when, and the who for each aspect of the PLC journey, the team will be better prepared to push those elements out to the school teams. To lead this process effectively, your guiding coalition may want to view its work through the lens of the basic PLC concepts. Does your team base its work on the three big ideas for the faculty (a focus on teacher learning, a focus on

Potential Look-Fors and Listen-Fors During Collaborative Team Meetings

All team members arrive on time.

All team members bring proper materials with them.

All team members have the same data source to view.

The meeting starts on time and ends on time.

The purpose of the meeting and the desired outcomes are stated.

A team agenda template or form is used.

Roles are mentioned, observed, or clarified (facilitator, recorder, participants, and so on).

Norms are referenced, written, and posted. (Ask for a copy.)

Norm violations are addressed.

One or more of the four critical questions are the focus of the team meeting.

Feedback Topics

Would you like feedback?

What does the team think went well?

What is one thing you would change or do differently the next time you meet?

Here are some positives I saw. (Follow with improvements to be considered: "You may wish to consider . . .")

Additional notes or comments:

FIGURE 2.4: Potential look-fors and listen-fors during collaborative team meetings and feedback topics.

*Visit **go.SolutionTree.com/PLCbooks** for a free reproducible version of this figure.*

a collaborative culture and collective responsibility for teachers, and a focus on results of the work of teachers to better meet students' needs and improve teachers' work)? Also, would your guiding coalition find it useful to adapt the four critical questions for its work? (What do we want our teacher teams to know and learn? How will we know if they've learned it? How will we respond if they have not learned it? How will we respond when teacher teams already know it?)

When collaborative teams pay close attention to the three big ideas and the four critical questions, your school will be on track to becoming a high-performing PLC. Learn and understand the process, lead and model the process, and monitor implementation of each step of the process to provide support and resources to those teams that need assistance. This learn, lead, model, and support pattern gives your school a path to successful schoolwide implementation. It may also be very beneficial for your guiding coalition to recognize teams that are enjoying success with the process and give them time during faculty meetings to share what they are doing in their collaborative team meetings. This way, other teams can learn their strategies.

Chapter 3, "Building a Solid PLC Foundation," will help you and your guiding coalition ensure that your PLC structure is rock solid. When the proper foundation is set and the correct structure is built, your school will be well on its way to becoming a high-functioning PLC.

▶ Next Steps

Have your guiding coalition complete the implementation fidelity assessment tool (figure 2.2, page 45). As a team, look at the collective responses, and discuss what is in place and how you can celebrate your progress in those areas. Then decide what actions and strategies are required to ensure that the guiding coalition and all collaborative teacher teams are staying true to the three big ideas. You might wish to use the three-step goal-setting process outlined in the following FAQs section to create action plans.

? FAQs

Is there a simple tool that can guide our guiding coalition to specifically focus on leading the three big ideas and four critical questions?

A simple three-step goal-setting process can help guide teams to successful outcomes by using results and data when responding to these three questions (Mwiya, 2015):

- Step 1—Where are you now?

- Step 2—Where do you want to be?

- Step 3—How will you get there?

Lead your guiding coalition through a discussion of the three big ideas and the four critical questions collectively or individually, whichever best meets the needs of your team. For example, if your guiding coalition is struggling with creating a clear focus on student learning, lead the team through the three-step process on how to intensify the school's focus on big idea 1.

- **Step 1:** Ask your team members where they believe the school currently is when it comes to the staff focusing on student learning. Is student learning job number one? If so, what evidence can your team share to support this response? What ideas might your team members share for celebrating the fact the school embraces student learning? If student learning is not a priority, what evidence can they share about where they believe the school is in making it a priority?

- **Step 2:** As a team, determine where your guiding coalition wants your school to be concerning big idea 1.

- **Step 3:** Once you have led your team through steps 1 and 2, have team members work together to develop their plan to ensure big idea 1 is a primary focus at your school.

Our guiding coalition has a good understanding of the PLC basics, and we are working well as a team. How do we take what we learn and experience in our guiding coalition and transfer those key learnings to our teams with consistency?

A benefit of leading your PLC journey through your guiding coalition is your school can use your guiding coalition like the food industry uses test kitchens or like the United States Air Force uses test pilots. With your guiding coalition, discuss a task in which your teams will engage. For example, when your teams are ready to answer critical question 1, "What do we want our students to learn?" have your guiding coalition practice the process of answering this question in your team meeting. Using a sample set of standards, go through a modified session to see what questions might arise, what aspects of the process may be confusing, and what ideas or strategies may prove useful in helping the team drill down to the essential standards. Learning and experiencing what their teachers go through will provide members of your guiding coalition with ideas and strategies for schoolwide consistency. Confidence and best practice can be the results of the testing done in your session.

Most of our collaborative learning teams are doing very well under the leadership of their guiding coalition members as they work their way through the four critical questions. I have two teams, however, that are struggling with the process. The first team is having difficulty responding to the four questions because the team leader is not as strong as most on the guiding coalition. The second team has a strong team leader, but the team has not completely bought into the whole idea of working collaboratively. Any advice on how to successfully lead these two teams?

To assist and support your weaker team leader, you may wish to attend a few of his or her team meetings to see if the structure and processes that lend themselves to successful collaboration are in place. Are team norms in place and being enforced? Does the team have an agenda that adds structure to the meetings and keeps them focused? Does the team leader have a good grasp of the basic concepts, or do you need to do some back-filling with that leader to boost his or her knowledge of the basics? Can another guiding coalition member observe and assist? Can your team leaders who need support sit in on a high-performing team meeting or two to see what successful team sessions look like? Finally, you may wish to bring the topic of successfully leading the PLC basics (three big ideas and four critical questions) back to the guiding coalition for review. Sharing what is going well and what stumbling blocks the leader has encountered and overcome could prove beneficial. Of course, you should share the weaker leader's situation in a way that honors his or her confidentiality and is considerate of his or her feelings.

Helping the second team leader, who leads a team that has not fully bought into the collaborative process, will take a different approach. First, that leader may wish to bring the challenge to a guiding coalition meeting for discussion and sharing of best practices. If the team leader has tried everything possible to lead productive sessions, to no avail, you may need to step in to assist the team. Such assistance can be provided by you, another administrator, or a resource person knowledgeable in leading the process to respond to the four critical questions. Is the team's behavior due to lack of knowledge of the basics, lack of understanding of the benefits of collaboration, or simply resistance? Depending on your observations, you will work with the team and team leader to get the team on track. If resistance is the issue, you will need to meet with the resisters individually to determine what the problem is and discuss how to resolve their concerns.

Our school is just beginning the PLC journey. As principal, I have bought into the concept of leading a school that embraces collaboration. How do I build the leadership capacity of my guiding coalition so it leads the PLC basics in the collaborative team meetings?

Every school starting the PLC journey faces this challenge to one degree or another. Aside from researching an extensive library of print and video resources on implementing PLC concepts, you may wish to review the AllThingsPLC website (www.allthings plc.info) for ideas and advice on how to effectively lead the PLC process and embed the PLC basics into your school's culture. In your professional learning library, you will want to include PLC at Work resources by authors like Rick DuFour, Becky DuFour, Bob Eaker, Thomas Many, Mike Mattos, Austin Buffum, Anthony Muhammad, Luis Cruz, Kim Bailey, Chris Jakicic, Timothy Kanold, Janel Keating, William Ferriter, Cassandra Erkens, and Eric Twadell, to name a few. These and other resources (such as those on RTI at Work) will provide you and your teams with the tools and information needed to guide you along your PLC journey. Especially helpful are the blog (www .allthingsplc.info/blog) and community forum (www.allthingsplc.info/forums) sections, where you and your guiding coalition can find answers to your questions and address the challenges that you will encounter.

Another excellent tool on the AllThingsPLC website is the PLC Locator (www.all thingsplc.info/plc-locator/us). This locator gives you access to information on Model PLC schools. These high-performing schools have demonstrated a commitment to the PLC concepts; implemented those concepts for at least three years; presented clear evidence of improved student learning; explained the culture, practices, and structures of the school or district; and submitted this information for the PLC review committee's consideration using an online submission process (AllThingsPLC, n.d.). To remain on the website as a nationally recognized model school, each school updates its information on the site to ensure it continues to meet the criteria of a national model school (AllThingsPLC, n.d.). The website includes information on each model school so that you and your team can contact model schools and learn how they met their challenges to implement PLC concepts.

As principal, I struggle at establishing a solid footing for the PLC basics in a school with high staff turnover. It seems we no sooner make positive headway in getting the staff on the same page and going in the same direction when we suffer from reductions in staff, transfers, or loss of resources. We seem to be in a constant state of starting over. How should I handle this challenge?

Highly effective schools have the capacity and potential to address the challenges and problems that they encounter. If you have not allowed your guiding coalition to discuss the ongoing turnover issue, you may want to consider it. Just because you are the principal does not mean that you come up with the solutions alone. You are, however, responsible for addressing this challenge; and perhaps the best way to do that is through your guiding coalition. The perspectives, ideas, and discussions may bear low-hanging fruit that can help your team, and eventually your PLC initiative, gain traction.

Another possible solution might be for your team to contact Model PLC schools that have experienced high turnover and learn how they dealt with it (see the information about the AllThingsPLC website in the previous answer). No school is alone on this journey. Whatever challenges your school faces have been experienced by other schools. Find those schools and contact them for ideas and strategies.

Reflection

Think about the role of the three big ideas and the four critical questions in your school and your collaborative teams' work together. Then complete the reproducible "Action Plan for Leading the PLC Basics" to plan how your guiding coalition can improve its leadership on the PLC basics.

Action Plan for Leading the PLC Basics

The Three Big Ideas	Evidence That Staff Understand the Big Idea	Evidence That the Big Idea Is Embedded in the School's Culture	Things the Guiding Coalition Can Do to Improve This
Big Idea 1: A focus on student learning			
Big Idea 2: A collaborative culture and collective responsibility			
Big Idea 3: A results orientation			
The Four Critical Questions	Evidence That Staff Understand the Critical Question	Evidence That the Critical Question Drives the Work of Collaborative Teams	Things the Guiding Coalition Can Do to Improve This
Critical Question 1: What do students need to know and be able to do?			
Critical Question 2: How will we know if they have learned it?			
Critical Question 3: How will we respond if they don't learn it?			
Critical Question 4: How will we extend the learning for those who have learned it?			

Source for big ideas and critical questions: DuFour, R., DuFour, R., Eaker, R., Many, T. W., & Mattos, M. (2016). Learning by doing: A handbook for Professional Learning Communities at Work *(3rd ed.). Bloomington, IN: Solution Tree Press.*

CHAPTER 3
BUILDING A SOLID PLC FOUNDATION

It is not the beauty of a building you should look at; it's the construction of the foundation that will stand the test of time.

—David Allan Coe

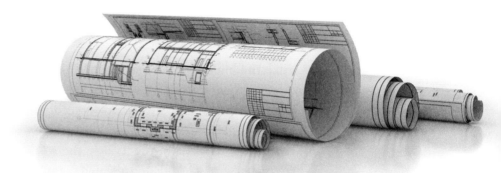

Traditionally led schools are filled with dedicated personnel who are extremely hardworking and have only the best interests of their students at heart. Although staff members are doing their very best with what they know, they often share a frustration—something is missing. The educators in traditional schools might think, "We're just not working hard enough, or working enough hours, or demanding enough of our students." Doing more is not the answer. These schools must do differently; the leaders within them must lead differently.

Traditionally led schools are not grounded by a stable, sturdy foundation. They seem to regularly change their direction and focus, searching for quick-fix solutions, programs of the month, and the latest and greatest slickly packaged resources guaranteed to raise student achievement in the shortest amount of time. They seek magic bullets to solve the needs and challenges that confront them. Every time political, financial, or social winds blow in a new direction, traditionally led schools weigh anchor and set sail for greener shores. But once they arrive, the greener shores have moved over the horizon, and the chase is on again. Instead of constantly looking for greener shores, high-performing principals and school leaders create their own green pastures by focusing on what they have control over: transforming the schools they serve.

The PLC process provides a green pasture that the entire school works to cultivate, beginning with the school leader and the guiding coalition. The process requires that schools build a strong foundation. Without a strong foundation, the PLC will eventually crumble—unable to withstand the inevitable challenges.

The Three School Structures

There are three basic school structures: traditional schools, pseudo-PLC schools, and PLC schools. Most schools have elements of all three types of schools on their campuses. For example, a high school might have a biology department that does not collaborate. The teachers are isolated. They do not share ideas, strategies, or best practice. They do not meet around the topic of student learning. This department operates as a department typically found in a traditional school.

The English II teachers, on the other hand, work as a collaborative team. A few of these teachers have worked in other schools that are true PLCs. They use their PLC experiences to focus on the big ideas and four critical questions. Their practices are found in true PLC schools.

Unlike the biology department, the fine arts department does meet occasionally. However, getting in the same room at the same time does not guarantee that teachers are being collaborative. When teachers talk about the details for the band, chorus, and drama classes going to see a production at the Civic Center, that discussion is important, but it does not rise to the level of the work and focus on collaborative practice. When teachers use scheduled, dedicated team time (which is precious to the PLC process) that does not focus on learning, they are working in a pseudo-PLC environment.

Understanding the differences among the three types of school structures is critical to creating a true PLC. Your guiding coalition should ask, "How is our school structured, and what must we do to ensure that we are organized and operating as a true PLC?"

Traditional Schools

The traditional school structure consists of a series of individual, independent classrooms with four walls, one teacher, and a closed door. Figure 3.1 shows the structure of a typical traditional elementary school: each grade level has multiple classrooms that operate as individual kingdoms. (If figure 3.1 showed a traditional secondary school's structure, the left column would be arranged by subject or content area—mathematics, science, social studies, band, physical education, and so on.) In traditionally structured schools, communication can be inefficient, sharing of best practices can be nonexistent, and student achievement generally stagnates. Principals of traditional schools often feel like they are being pulled in many directions at the same time. Traditional school structures tend to flounder because much of their organization and processes do not allow for collaborative practice.

The W. Edwards Deming (W. Edwards Deming Institute, 2015) quote, "A bad system will beat a good person every single time," describes the impact of structures that do not allow for collaborative practices. One power the guiding coalition has is the ability to build new structures and systems that can erase ineffective systems and processes (Saddington, 2016).

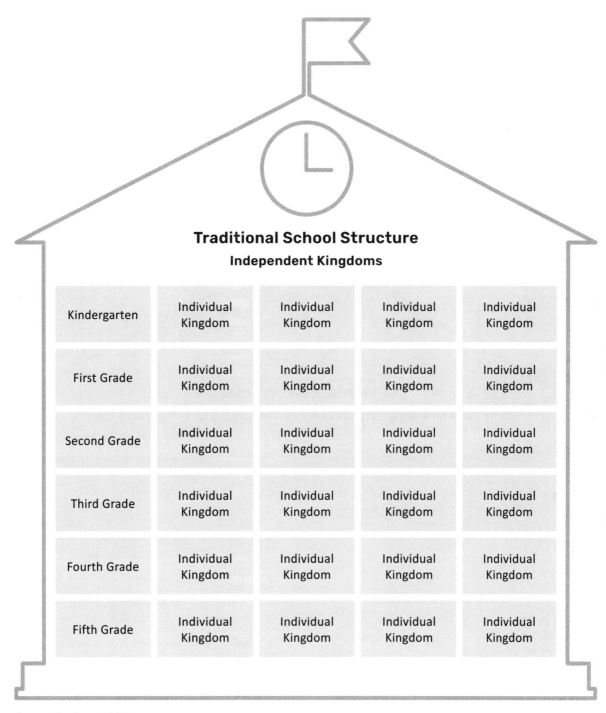

Traditional School Structure
Independent Kingdoms

Kindergarten	Individual Kingdom	Individual Kingdom	Individual Kingdom	Individual Kingdom
First Grade	Individual Kingdom	Individual Kingdom	Individual Kingdom	Individual Kingdom
Second Grade	Individual Kingdom	Individual Kingdom	Individual Kingdom	Individual Kingdom
Third Grade	Individual Kingdom	Individual Kingdom	Individual Kingdom	Individual Kingdom
Fourth Grade	Individual Kingdom	Individual Kingdom	Individual Kingdom	Individual Kingdom
Fifth Grade	Individual Kingdom	Individual Kingdom	Individual Kingdom	Individual Kingdom

Source: DuFour, 2015.

FIGURE 3.1: Traditional school structure.

Pseudo PLCs

Another type of school structure is the pseudo-PLC structure (also called PLC lite [DuFour et al., 2016]). It is a false PLC structure because it does not have all the required elements of a true PLC. As shown in figure 3.2 (page 60), the classroom walls in each grade level or department are opened up, allowing for collaboration and improved communication, but there are no guarantees such teamwork exists. Teachers are generally grouped by grade level or subject matter; but for all intents and purposes, they remain largely isolated because they are grouped by name only. These groups usually meet infrequently, and when they do meet, they have little if any real focus on the work of greatest importance—student learning. Conversations tend to be unfocused and don't address the real work that needs to be done.

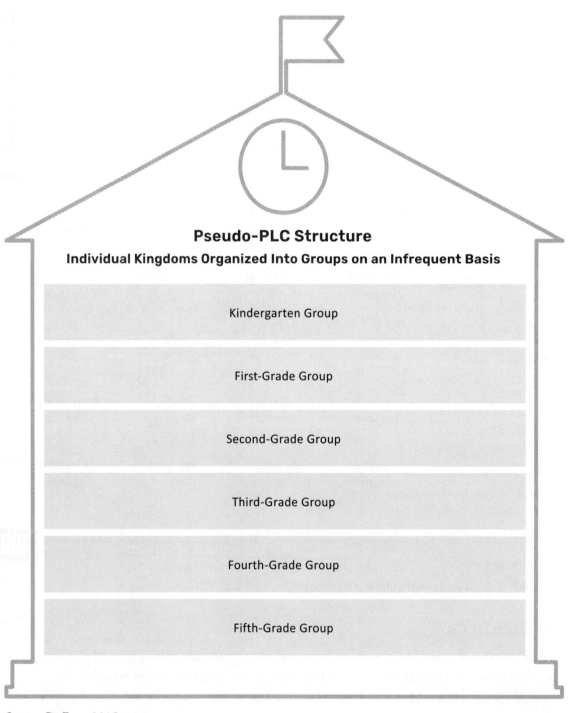

Pseudo-PLC Structure

Individual Kingdoms Organized Into Groups on an Infrequent Basis

Kindergarten Group

First-Grade Group

Second-Grade Group

Third-Grade Group

Fourth-Grade Group

Fifth-Grade Group

Source: DuFour, 2015.

FIGURE 3.2: Pseudo-PLC structure.

Pseudo PLCs can be dangerous because the educators within them falsely believe that by operating as a grade-level or department-level team, they are working as a PLC. After working as a pseudo PLC, frustration and tension may set in. Why? Because teams see no substantive results from their reorganization. Principals of pseudo PLCs who seek the very best for their students and staff eventually conclude that something needs to be done differently. They look around and notice that schools very similar to theirs are achieving at incredible levels. How can that be? Their teachers are working as hard as ever yet seem to be spinning their wheels. When they look closer, they learn that although their schools appear to be similar to the higher-performing schools, looks are deceiving. The staffs of the higher-performing schools work and behave differently—they are true PLCs.

True PLCs

True PLCs are different from traditional and pseudo-PLC schools because of the foundation upon which they operate (DuFour et al., 2016). True PLCs are guided by three big ideas: (1) a focus on learning, (2) a collaborative culture and collective responsibility, and (3) a results orientation. They have four foundational pillars: (1) mission, (2) vision, (3) values (collective commitments), and (4) goals. And collaborative teams work in cycles of continuous improvement to answer four critical questions: (1) What knowledge, skills, and dispositions should every student acquire as a result of this unit, this course, or this grade level? (2) How will we know when each student has acquired the essential knowledge and skills? (3) How will we respond when some students do not learn? and (4) How will we extend the learning for students who are already proficient? The rest of this chapter explores the creation and structure of true PLCs.

PLC Creation

Stephen Covey (1989) writes that all things are created twice. The first creation is the mental blueprint of what is to be built—what you want after thinking everything through. The second creation comes from putting the plans into physical form. For example, think about what you are sitting on right now. Someone first thought about the design, the structure, the materials, and the process to create the seat before turning those plans into a comfortable place to sit. Your clothes, your home, your car, your computer, your streamed movies, your favorite brewed coffee and the cup it's in, ad infinitum—these things were created in someone's mind before they were constructed and took physical form.

PLCs are created in the same way. They start as a mental blueprint involving the school principal and the guiding coalition, and from the blueprint, the physical form evolves. When the principal and guiding coalition share PLC concepts and processes with others in the building, interest and support increase around the concept of building capacity to create a better way of working together.

The process of successfully becoming a PLC gradually builds momentum and capacity over time. It is a slow, messy process. Schools often take two steps forward and three steps back. The process of becoming a fully functioning PLC is *learning by doing*. It doesn't happen by extensive research. It's not learning by setting up committees. It's not learning by waiting for a new board or superintendent. It's not learning by delaying everything until the new school year starts or until you get more funds or until everyone on staff falls in love with the idea. The process requires rolling up your sleeves and starting. Before long, there will be a groundswell of professional learning and best practice. Implementation of PLC concepts will sustain a school culture where student learning is the top priority, where teachers work collaboratively with collective responsibility, and where the focus on results helps teams make decisions that are in the best interest of students. In true PLCs, best practice becomes common practice.

Plan and Prepare the PLC Construction Site

Before a foundation is poured, a great deal of planning and preparation must occur in advance. This prep work cannot be rushed. It takes time and attention to detail to build the foundation properly and according to the plans. The site or footprint is surveyed. If needed, excavation levels the ground. Footings create structural bases that evenly spread the building's weight for solid support. The design of the foundation is laid out using forms. Once the preliminary work is complete, the foundation's concrete is poured. When the foundation is completely hardened, the forms used to hold the wet concrete are stripped away, leaving a strong, well-built foundation (Jason, n.d.).

Before building the PLC foundation, similar preparation takes place. Building a PLC without advance prep work and foundation setting would be similar to building a home on an uneven base of soft soil and shifting sand. A foundation rushed is a foundation ruined. It takes far more time and resources to fix a faulty, poorly laid foundation than it does to proceed cautiously and deliberately in the first place. Before teacher teams begin their collaborative work, a school must spend time on the first creation. The engineering team for this planning and preparation is the guiding coalition.

Not all building sites are the same. Many factors contribute to the decision on how to proceed at every construction location. Some structures go up relatively quickly because the ground is solid and can easily support the new building. Few resources are spent to prepare these sites because very minimal preparation is required. Some sites, however, require massive planning and preparation before the first shovelful of dirt is turned. Costly planning may be needed. Additional experts may need to be consulted to help solve the myriad of problems and challenges that the construction team faces. Each location presents its unique challenges for the builder.

The same is true for schools. Not all schools are the same. Some schools become PLCs with little time and little effort because conditions are perfect for teacher collaboration. Few problems get in the way of implementation of PLC concepts and processes. Other schools find the effort to create a collaborative culture to be daunting, extremely difficult, and perhaps disappointing.

Like buildings, PLCs can be created in every school regardless of their location, their conditions, and the populations they serve. Contributing factors to whether schools will become high-performing PLCs, regardless of their makeup, demographics, or achievement levels, may well be found in the commitment, determination, resilience, and grit of their principals and the guiding coalitions they lead (Hoerr, 2017).

Before constructing the foundation of a new building, the site needs to be properly prepared. If an existing building is being renovated, the architect, contractor, or builder ensures the site is suitable to support the upgraded structure. If it is not suitable, it has to be brought up to code before changes to the foundation and structure can be made.

Before building a PLC in a brand-new school, you and your guiding coalition properly prepare the "cultural site" on which your PLC foundation will be constructed. If you are transforming an existing school into a PLC, you and your guiding coalition will first assess whether your school is ready and capable of supporting a collaborative culture. Regardless of where your school is in the PLC process, the soil has to be prepared and the footings must be dug before the foundation can be built. Are the cultural footings and the PLC foundation stable enough to support the weight of the new construction?

Set the Cultural Footings

All schools have a culture, whether public, private, charter, large, small, rural, or urban. The bad news for students and staff is that many of those cultures are toxic or have pockets of toxicity. It is the school leader's responsibility to ensure that the culture is a thriving, positive, nurturing one in which all students and staff are safe, valued, and successful.

Before your guiding coalition can lead the PLC foundation building, it ensures the ground on which your PLC will rest is properly prepared and can accept the cultural footings that will ultimately support the foundation. A strong, well-built building is of little value or use if it has a weak, faulty, and unsafe foundation.

In a PLC, the foundation is formed "when a school commits to creating consensus in four critical areas. These are the four pillars of a PLC at Work" (DuFour et al., 2021, p. 83; see figure 3.3, page 64):

1. **Shared mission:** Why do we exist?

2. **Shared vision:** What do we hope to become?

3. **Shared values:** What commitments must we make to create the school or district that will improve our ability to fulfill our purpose?

4. **Shared goals:** What goals will we use to monitor our progress? (DuFour et al., 2021, p. 83)

Keating and colleagues (2008) suggest the following actions take place before the PLC foundation is created. In construction terminology, these actions could be viewed as the footings that support the foundation, as outlined in figure 3.4 (page 65). Setting

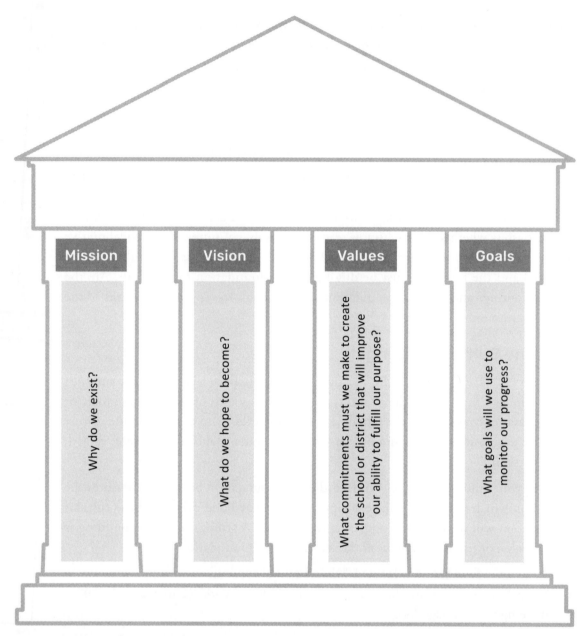

Source: DuFour et al., 2021, p. 84.

FIGURE 3.3: The four pillars of a PLC at Work.

the following footings will help distribute the weight of the developing PLC. Without setting these footings firmly in place, PLC initiatives run the risk of collapsing.

- Build shared knowledge of PLC characteristics and their links to the research of effective schooling practices.
- Build shared knowledge of the current reality in your district or school.
- Develop a guiding coalition.
- Establish a common vocabulary.
- Celebrate your progress on the PLC journey.

PLC Foundation The four pillars of a PLC	PLC Footings The five actions that help create and strengthen the PLC's collaborative culture
Definition: The foundation is the structure that helps support the weight of the PLC. The PLC foundation rests directly on the PLC footings. The foundation can be compared to legs.	Definition: The PLC footings support the PLC foundation. The culture is made up of "long-held assumptions, beliefs, expectations, and habits" and illustrates "the way we do things around here" (DuFour & Fullan, 2013, p. 2). Footings create the stability for the pillars.
Pillar 1: Mission answers the question, "Why do we exist?"	Footing 1: Build shared knowledge of PLC characteristics and their links to the research of effective schooling practices.
Pillar 2: Vision answers the question, "What do we hope to become?"	Footing 2: Build shared knowledge of the current reality in your district or school.
Pillar 3: Values (collective commitments) answer the question, "What commitments must we make to create the school or district that will improve our ability to fulfill our purpose?" "How do we promise to behave?"	Footing 3: Develop a guiding coalition.
Pillar 4: Goals answer the question, "What goals will we use to monitor our progress?"	Footings 4 and 5: Establish a common vocabulary, and celebrate your progress on the PLC journey.

Source: Adapted from Bhuiyan, n.d.

FIGURE 3.4: Pillars and footings of a PLC.

As leadership and staff learn together, several cultural benefits, such as teamwork, empowerment, and collaboration, evolve and strengthen. When your school rallies around the basic concepts of working together for the benefit of improved achievement for all students, trust, communication, and risk taking increase. Under your leadership, this laser-like focus creates the opportunity for your teams to work together and see the results of their collective efficacy, the shared belief that together they can and will make a difference (Kaplan & Owings, 2013). Nothing can be more fulfilling or professionally satisfying than that.

There is no correct order to the actions in the following sections. Where you begin will depend on your leadership style, your school's organizational structure, and your staff's readiness and receptiveness for change. What is most important is that all five actions must be completed. The quality of the work that is made in these five initial steps will determine the quality, durability, and success of your PLC. Footings that are properly set will support and strengthen the foundation.

Build Shared Knowledge of PLC Characteristics and Their Links to the Research of Effective Schooling Practices

School leaders need to ensure all staff members learn the basic PLC characteristics and concepts as part of the first steps to becoming a PLC. Research-based information and links to effective practices will help staff answer the question, "What is this thing called a PLC that we are about to pursue?" Generally, organizations begin new initiatives with a compelling why before outlining the details of the what.

Build Shared Knowledge of the Current Reality in Your District or School

Faculty members must have a clear understanding of where the school or district is with data over time. Without data, you are just a person with an opinion (Jones & Silberzahn, 2016). To build this shared knowledge, schools look at information that may include student achievement data, attendance, tardies, suspensions, graduation rates, perception assessments, and demographic information (DuFour et al., 2016). Figure 3.5 will help your guiding coalition collect and compare your school data in a number of areas. These types of data paint a picture of the school's current status. Data that scream, "This needs attention! Now! Immediately! Do not pass go!" will help determine where collaborative teams will begin their focus.

Develop a Guiding Coalition

The most critical action a principal can take is the creation and development of the school's guiding coalition. This guiding coalition or leadership team becomes the team that provides advice and support to the principal and assists in leading the PLC initiative. Without a formal guiding coalition, successful implementation and embedding of the PLC concepts into the school's culture will be virtually impossible.

Traditional schools with established leadership teams seldom dedicate their resources to ensuring all students learn; instead, they generally focus on daily management responsibilities such as budgets, schedules, operations, maintenance, policies, and so on (Buffum et al., 2018).

Many school leaders allow teachers to work however they choose. Teachers may partner with another teacher or two. They may work alone. Teachers in one grade level or department may have several different goals or targets for their students despite being responsible for the same curriculum. These school leaders may focus more on compliance, rules, and structure. Managerial functions are essential and cannot be ignored; however, accomplishing managerial tasks is a fraction of what needs to be accomplished in our schools. If ensuring students learn at high levels is the main purpose of school, school leadership does more than merely "run" the school. It leads the learning. The best way to lead the learning is through the guiding coalition.

Establish a Common Vocabulary

To best communicate concepts, processes, and information with all staff members, understanding PLC terms and their definitions is critical. All terms should have the

A Data Picture of Our School

School Name:

Student Achievement Results

Indicator	Year 20___-20___	Year 20___-20___	Year 20___-20___	Facts About Our Data
Based on Our School Assessment Data				
Based on Our District Assessment Data				
Based on Our State or Provincial Assessment Data				
Based on Our National Assessment Data				

Student Engagement Data

Average Daily Attendance				
Percentage of Students in Extracurricular Activities				
Percentage of Students Using School's Tutoring Services				
Percentage of Students Enrolled in Most Rigorous Courses Offered				
Percentage of Students Graduating Without Retention				
Percentage of Students Who Drop Out of School				

FIGURE 3.5: A data picture of our school.

continued →

A Data Picture of Our School

Student Engagement Data (continued)

Indicator	Year 20__–20__	Year 20__–20__	Year 20__–20__	Facts About Our Data
Other Areas in Which We Hope to Engage Students, Such as Community Service				

Discipline

	Year 20__–20__	Year 20__–20__	Year 20__–20__	Facts About Our Data
Number of Referrals / Top Three Reasons for Referrals				
Number of Parent Conferences Regarding Discipline				
Number of In-School Suspensions				
Number of Detentions / Saturday School				
Number of Out-of-School Suspensions				
Number of Expulsions				
Other				

Survey Data

	Year 20__–20__	Year 20__–20__	Year 20__–20__	Facts About Our Data
Student Satisfaction or Perception Assessment				
Alumni Satisfaction or Perception Assessment				

A Data Picture of Our School

Survey Data (continued)

Indicator	Year 20___–20___	Year 20___–20___	Year 20___–20___	Facts About Our Data
Parent Satisfaction or Perception Assessment				
Teacher Satisfaction or Perception Assessment				
Administration Satisfaction or Perception Assessment				
Community Satisfaction or Perception Assessment				

Demographic Data

Percent Free and Reduced Lunch				
Percent Mobility				
Percent Special Education				
Percent English as a Second Language				
Percent White (Not of Hispanic Origin)				
Percent Black				
Percent Hispanic				
Percent Asian				
Percent Native American				

Source: DuFour et al., 2016, pp. 29–31.
*Visit **go.SolutionTree.com/PLCbooks** for a free reproducible version of this figure.*

same meaning to all staff members. When terms are misused or misunderstood, it is the responsibility of the guiding coalition members to correct this problem on their collaborative teams. Through the use of a common vocabulary, it is possible to have conversations, solve problems, and make decisions that prove to be productive and beneficial. When confusion and misunderstanding exist, success is in jeopardy. As Mike Schmoker (2004) notes, "Clarity precedes competence" (p. 85).

The guiding coalition, under the principal's leadership, should become familiar with the basic PLC terms and definitions. This team can easily learn the language of PLCs through book studies of publications like *Learning by Doing* (DuFour et al., 2016), *Concise Answers to Frequently Asked Questions About Professional Learning Communities at Work* (Mattos et al., 2016), and *Revisiting Professional Learning Communities at Work* (DuFour et al., 2021). Visit **go.SolutionTree .com/PLCbooks** to download a PLC glossary.

Participating in Solution Tree PLC at Work summits, events, and other professional learning opportunities is another great way to become familiar with PLC terms and definitions and their application to leading the establishment of a consistently used vocabulary. The guiding coalition is responsible for ensuring the correct use of terms and holding collaborative team members accountable when they misuse them.

At the school level, professional learning sessions specifically focused on the proper use of PLC terms and definitions with examples and non-examples could prove helpful for the guiding coalition. Included in such sessions could be strategies on how to model the proper use of terminology and how to effectively ensure its use schoolwide.

Principals can also place time on a guiding coalition agenda for the team members to share how they are successfully embedding PLC terms and definitions into their collaborative team meetings. They could also share barriers they encounter so that the guiding coalition can discuss ways to overcome those barriers.

Celebrate Your Progress on the PLC Journey

PLC experts have witnessed a shortcoming that is common to many schools: the lack of attention to meaningful celebration. School staffs work tirelessly, and the majority of faculty and staff members do amazing work with students, with each other, and with parents and the community. Here are some questions about celebration for you and your guiding coalition to consider: Do you regularly celebrate individual and team efforts? Are recognition and celebration part of your school's culture? Do staff members celebrate their successes? If the answers to any of these questions include "no," "not really," or "not as much as we should," then celebration should become a priority for the guiding coalition. In a PLC, the most important celebrations focus on celebrating teams and team accomplishments. Tom Peters, coauthor of the book *A Passion for Excellence: The Leadership Difference* (Peters & Austin, 1985), reminds leaders to "celebrate what you want to see more of" (RightAttitudes.com, n.d.).

An elementary principal once shared with me that she was not a big believer in recognitions and celebrations. She was proud of being referred to as the "data queen" of her district, and she was very good at using data to drive decisions at her school. She shared that she did not have a celebratory bone in her body and saw little value in wasting time celebrating when that time could be used to work on the next goal for the school.

My response to her was that as the principal, you may not personally create and facilitate all the celebrations and recognitions at your school; however, it is your responsibility, as the school leader, to make sure that celebration, motivation, and inspiration frequently take place. You don't have to plan or lead the celebrations yourself. Allow others to play to their strengths and contribute to ensure recognition of team efforts is accomplished.

Figure 3.6 is a survey that might help your guiding coalition assess the impact and status of your school's celebration and recognition of team efforts.

Celebration and Recognition Survey			
Elements of Celebration and Recognition	Current Status (Circle *yes* if the element is in place in your school. Circle *no* if the element is not in place.)		Evidence or Required Action (If yes, what evidence is there? If no, what actions must you take?)
Does your school formally plan celebration and recognition of team efforts?	Yes	No	
If so, are teachers included in planning and conducting the celebrations?	Yes	No	
Are adequate resources made available to support recognition and celebration of team efforts?	Yes	No	
If you have teams that receive a disproportionate amount of recognition or celebration, do you have plans to spread recognition and celebration more evenly among your teams? Do you have plans to ensure all teams will be recognized some time during the school year?	Yes	No	
If a visitor to your school were to walk the empty campus, would he or she be able to determine what your school recognizes or celebrates? Would he or she be able to determine what you value?	Yes	No	

FIGURE 3.6: Celebration and recognition survey.

*Visit **go.SolutionTree.com/PLCbooks** for a free reproducible version of this figure.*

Stephen Covey once asked this question: "Have you ever been so busy driving that you forgot to stop and get gas?" (FranklinCovey, 2017). Teachers, staff, and administrators are so busy and so focused on their work that many times they forget to stop to fill their emotional fuel tanks. Celebrating the good work and success of teams sustains the PLC and ensures it continues its forward momentum.

The PLC Structure

An important question often arises when schools begin the process of becoming a PLC: "How do we get buy-in or ownership from everyone on staff?" Striving for unanimity during such transformational work may prove to be most unrealistic. Waiting for every staff member to agree to and embrace any change effort can significantly slow down the process. As schools begin their journeys, they do not wait for 100 percent buy-in or ownership. Leaders should not wait for every teacher to embrace working in teams before they take the first step. If they do, they'll never move forward with becoming a PLC. Few groups naturally collaborate. They will need resources, tools, support, and time to learn how to work together. By changing behaviors first, principals witness attitudes change and observe teachers becoming more receptive to collaboration. "Go with those who are on board with the concept. Start somewhere and build your foundation with the people you have. Momentum, excitement, interest, and improved results will follow" (Hall, 2012).

School leaders and guiding coalitions must first address and clarify what a PLC is. Once the guiding coalition understands key terms and definitions, members can more easily share this information with collaborative teams. Learning the why comes before answering the what, when, and how.

Figure 3.7 is a helpful graphic to show guiding coalition and staff members how a PLC is structured.

It is this foundation that separates traditionally structured schools and pseudo-PLC schools from true PLCs. There are four pillars to the PLC foundation: (1) mission, (2) vision, (3) values (collective commitments), and (4) goals. PLCs must have all four pillars solidly in place before moving to the collaborative work.

The Four Pillars

The following sections explore the four pillars of a PLC in more detail.

Mission

On September 12, 1962, President John F. Kennedy inspired a nation in the sweltering heat at the Rice University football stadium with his speech on the United States' space effort (his "Moon Speech"). On that historic day, President Kennedy charged the United States with an extremely challenging mission: to land a man on the moon and bring him safely back to earth (Kettley, 2019). On July 24, 1969, the United States accomplished that mission.

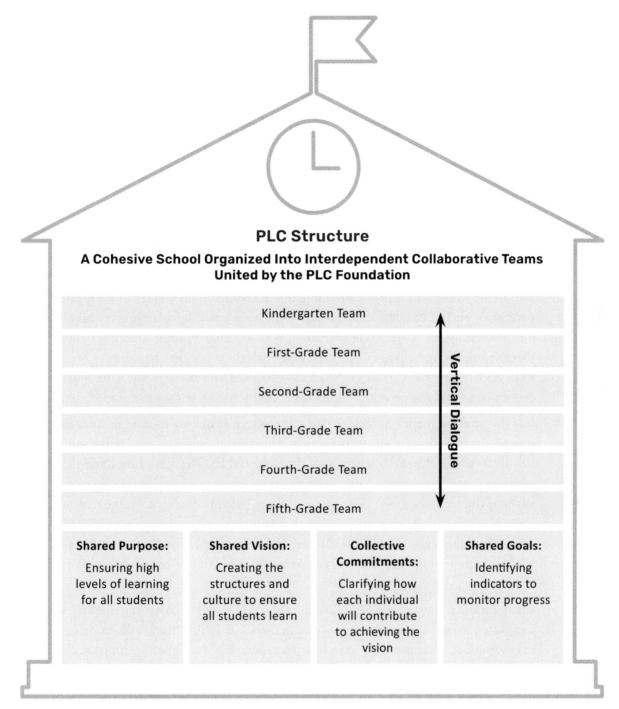

PLC Structure

A Cohesive School Organized Into Interdependent Collaborative Teams United by the PLC Foundation

Kindergarten Team

First-Grade Team

Second-Grade Team

Third-Grade Team

Fourth-Grade Team

Fifth-Grade Team

Vertical Dialogue

Shared Purpose:	**Shared Vision:**	**Collective Commitments:**	**Shared Goals:**
Ensuring high levels of learning for all students	Creating the structures and culture to ensure all students learn	Clarifying how each individual will contribute to achieving the vision	Identifying indicators to monitor progress

Source: DuFour, 2015.

FIGURE 3.7: PLC structure.

Why did they fly to the moon? Although the mission was more political than scientific at the time, the Apollo program challenged Americans to imagine and do the impossible, to think beyond what they believed they were capable of doing. President Kennedy's words, "We choose to go to the moon," were not as much about flying to a distant heavenly body as they were about testing man's limits and accomplishing something so "out of this world" that Americans would reap immeasurable benefits as a result. Had President Kennedy not laid out the mission, it would have taken much longer to accomplish this once seemingly unimaginable feat.

Your school's mission can accomplish the same focus, inspiration, and impact that Kennedy's mission did for the country in 1962. A school's mission describes the school's purpose. It answers the question, "Why do we exist?" If your school currently has a mission statement, the guiding coalition will want to review the mission and ask, "Does our current mission statement describe why we exist?" If the current mission does not adequately describe why the school exists, give the fundamental purpose, or clarify the priorities and sharpen the focus of the school, it is to be rewritten.

The guiding coalition initiates the review process. Taking an existing mission to the entire school staff first can create some formidable obstacles. Those who served on the team to write the current mission might take offense that their product was insufficient or that they did something wrong. Depending on the culture, taking the current mission to the whole staff for review, comments, and suggestions could cause a great deal of confusion. Should building common knowledge about the forthcoming transformations not be established, there could be many questions and misunderstandings about why there should be any changes and tinkering with the work that has already been done. PLC leaders will want to keep the process focused and manageable. The best way to do this is to start the process with review and discussion within the guiding coalition.

If the guiding coalition decides that the mission is not up-to-date or does not adequately describe the purpose of the school, the guiding coalition members should write the mission with the entire school staff. Experienced PLC leaders understand that every adult on campus serves students. Schools are much more than a gathering of teachers; without the personnel who clean the buildings, provide meals, assist the teachers, and provide all the other essential services that students and staff require, PLC structures cannot possibly exist (DuFour, DuFour, & Eaker, 2008). For these reasons, you may wish to include support personnel in the creation of your mission, vision, and values.

Once the mission statement process is complete, the guiding coalition should answer the question, "How do we bring life to the words in our mission statement?" Posting laminated mission and vision statements does not ensure they will set direction or inspire action. A great way to learn how successful PLCs use their missions to drive the work, inspire the staff, and serve as the motivation to focus on student learning is to contact Model PLCs for ideas, tips, and suggestions. (You can use the AllThingsPLC website's PLC Locator for this purpose; see chapter 2, page 37.) You will most likely learn what not to do and how not to do it based on their failures and missteps. Their experiences will prove invaluable and help increase the impact of your school's mission. You might also consider looking into how business and industry use their mission and vision statements to inspire and set direction. Filter your mission statement through the question, "Does our mission statement answer this question, 'Why do we exist?'" If the answer is yes, your mission is good to go. If the answer is no or probably not, the guiding coalition should consider updating the mission.

Voices From the Field

I didn't believe in the simple things in the beginning. We didn't bother with norm, vision, or mission building. We jumped right into the work of team meetings and common assessments without establishing the why. I assumed adults knew how to work together and they would be as excited about the work as I was. Neither turned out to be true. We had to backtrack after two years of floundering and start from the beginning. I could have saved us some time and stress if I had known that up front.

—Middle School Principal, Missouri

Vision

During the 1980s, Jimmy Valvano was North Carolina State University's head basketball coach. Early in his first season, the NC State Wolfpack hit the court prepared for practice. To the players' surprise, something was very different about this practice and this coach. There was not a basketball in sight. Basketball practice without basketballs? Valvano gathered his new team around him and brashly announced that they were going to win the national championship. They were an average team at best, and they were going to do what? (Hock, 2013).

Although basketballs were absent that day, there was something under the basket at the far end of the court: a ladder. The coach walked his players to the ladder and told them if they followed him, worked hard, worked as a team, and trusted each other, they would become national champions. He had his team climb the ladder one by one. With a gold pair of scissors, each player cut off a piece of the net. Cutting down the basketball net symbolized a championship win. After each player cut off a piece, Valvano climbed the ladder and cut off the final piece, raised it above his head, and cheered as if the team had just won the national championship. That was Valvano's dream, his vision. At the time, many probably thought this was crazy talk by a crazy coach. However, at the end of the 1983 NCAA basketball championship, the Wolfpack climbed the champions' ladder to victoriously cut down the nets and celebrate one of the most fantastic championship runs in collegiate sports history (Hock, 2013).

Thurl Bailey, center for the Wolfpack's national championship team, sums up the powerful vision that Valvano created:

> The more he spoke, the more we sat up, the more we listened. He painted a
> picture for us. He said, "If I can get you to see what I see, what I'm seeing,
> the dream that I'm dreaming, we can get there." (Hock, 2013)

To demonstrate the power and importance of vision, you might wish to try the following activity with your guiding coalition or faculty.

1. Begin by standing and spreading out to give members room for this exercise.

2. Ask team members to look at any fixed object at the other side of the room and then extend their arms out to the side at shoulder height. Keeping their head still, they should horizontally turn their extended arms in one direction (left or right) until they feel some resistance and tension. Team members should keep their eyes fixed on the object—no turning of heads. Ask members, "Notice how far you turn. Now turn your arms in the opposite direction. Do not strain or overextend yourself as you turn. Again, notice how far you turned. Drop your arms to your sides. Your movements should have felt limited and restricted."

3. Next, ask team members, "Now hold your arms out to the side at shoulder height. This time, have your eyes and head lead your turn. Turn your head, arms, shoulders, and trunk in one direction. Now turn in the opposite direction. Did you turn greater distances than when your gaze was fixed?" The lesson behind this simple exercise is that when you follow your vision, your organization will go further than when you do not have a vision or you do not follow your current vision.

A school's vision answers the question, "What do we want our school to become?" The vision review and revision process is similar to the mission process. The main difference is that while the mission is created with the entire staff, the vision is created by staff representatives. These representatives could exclusively be the guiding coalition or select guiding coalition members. The vision creation team could be an ad hoc committee whose purpose is to create the vision based on the mission work and with input from the staff. Once its preliminary work is complete, this ad hoc team would present the vision draft to the staff for review and input. This review and input-gathering phase can be done with the whole staff or by the guiding coalition members with each of their collaborative teams. Based on team input and suggestions, the ad hoc team can then revise the original draft and send it out or present it one more time for final review and approval.

As with the mission, once the vision is created, the guiding coalition will want to discuss how that vision will be used throughout the school year. How will your school live the vision each day? What will your "cutting the nets down" look like and feel like? How will your guiding coalition lead your school to see your school's vision and realize your school's dream for all students?

Having a vision does not guarantee a national championship, higher student achievement, or a successful PLC. However, without vision, members of organizations are likely to become discouraged because their hard work seems to be getting them nowhere. Without a clear, unified vision, staff members may become divided as a result of developing their pictures of what success will look like. Competing pictures of success can cause confusion and disagreement. Organizations that have no vision are like trains without tracks. Derailment is disastrous (Price, 2019). "Where there is no vision, the people perish" (*King James Bible*, n.d., Proverbs 29:18). In schools where there is no vision, momentum dies. The focus on student learning dims. Progress stalls and motivation stagnates.

The development and implementation of the organizational vision is one of the most critical yet overlooked aspects of high-performing PLCs. There is a reason a car's windshield is many times bigger than the rearview mirrors. When schools create their vision, embed it into their culture, and follow it, all things are possible and endless opportunities lie ahead. When schools recognize the power and possibility that their vision can create, it is as if they are looking through a large windshield at the exciting journey that lies ahead. This focus on the future helps put old habits, harmful past practice, and "the way we used to do things" in the rearview mirror. Anything seen in the rearview mirror gets smaller and smaller until it eventually disappears from sight.

Values (Collective Commitments)

While all four pillars are critical, pillar 3, values (collective commitments), may be the least understood and least used, yet the most powerful of the four. Values or collective commitments answer the question, "What commitments must we make to create the school or district that will improve our ability to fulfill our purpose?" Collective commitments become the promises staff members make with their colleagues and fellow staff members on how they will act and how they will treat each other.

The work to create this essential pillar is similar to the vision creation process, where the guiding coalition or an ad hoc committee leads the drafting of a set of values for staff input and review. The same team that led the vision process can do the work; or, to widen the school's leadership capacity, a separate team can lead the values work.

The power in this pillar lies in how the collective commitments are used. Here are sample collective commitments based on the organizational values of Brevard Public Schools (2021) in Viera, Florida (where the author was director of educational leadership and professional development). Notice these commitments or values are written as *we will* statements.

- We will make decisions based on what is in the best interest of all students.
- We will uphold honesty and integrity as our guiding principles.
- We will treat others with respect.
- We will set high expectations and demand quality performance.
- We will take responsibility for our actions and be accountable for the results.
- We will foster a safe, accessible, and healthy environment.
- We will value diversity and the strength of individual differences.
- We will provide a positive, caring, and supportive climate.
- We will work as a team to accomplish our mission.

As with all the foundational pillars of a PLC, words without action have no meaning or purpose. Imagine these sample collective commitments are your school's. Imagine that an ad hoc committee or perhaps your entire staff developed these values; revised them after review and input; had them approved by the entire staff by consensus; and had them printed, published, and posted. As principal, you have the responsibility to use these collective commitments as the lens through which you view the actions and behaviors of staff members. As you go through your day, you constantly watch and listen for actions that embody the school's collective commitments. These values give you a positive lens to see how people behave. They are not a set of rules or a list of gotchas. Rather, as the school leader, you should be constantly observing to identify individuals who are living and breathing these commitments. The following example shows how you can use these sample collective commitments powerfully.

As you walk the halls before school begins, you notice one of your teachers, Candice, speaking with a concerned parent in the hallway outside her room. Her eye contact, her body language, and her empathic listening skills catch your attention. The parent is noticeably agitated, but Candice acknowledges and legitimizes the concerns. Her manner and voice have a calming effect. As you pass, you make a mental note to speak with Candice later in the day. When you get back to the office, you leave her a note to see you after school.

That afternoon, you meet with Candice and remind her of the school's collective commitments and that she was part of the process to create them. You draw her attention to the third value in the list, "We will treat others with respect." You share with her your observation of her impromptu conversation in the hallway that morning. You let her know that she was the embodiment of the third collective commitment. You let her know how much you appreciate her modeling the commitments for students and staff. You thank her for being such a great member of the team.

Daily celebrations such as this accomplish several things. First, Candice feels terrific! What a way to end the day! Second, you feel terrific. You looked at behaviors and actions through a positive lens. Complimenting Candice was an uplifting experience for both of you—what Covey (1989) calls a double deposit in both emotional bank accounts. Finally, word gets around that you value and appreciate the work that staff members do to embody the school's values.

When recognizing individuals for what you see, keep the message private and personal. When recognizing teams for modeling the values, consider recognizing them publicly. Thank staff members, and let them know how much you appreciate their efforts. If you have time, a personal note is a good idea. It might end up on a refrigerator next to their children's or grandchildren's artwork or in a desk drawer or on a bulletin board where it can serve as motivation during bumpy or tough times.

Part of being aware of when staff members embody collective commitments is noticing when they do not. Another teacher, Ray, is speaking with a parent over the phone in a small office adjoining the main reception area. There are parents, students, and teachers in the office. The conversation is heated. Ray's voice rises. The comments become personal. The call ends with Ray slamming the phone down and storming out of the office. One of your office staff shares with you the details of the incident. You send Ray an email asking that he stop by before he leaves for the day.

As you did with Candice, you welcome Ray in and remind him of the school's collective commitments and that he was part of the process to develop and approve them. You tell him, "Ray, as you know, one of our values is, 'We will treat others with respect.'" You go on to let him know that you learned the details about the emotional outburst overheard in the office. You let him know that he violated the school's collective commitment about respect. You continue the conversation to learn more from Ray about what happened and why it happened. You speak with him about future situations that will occur and what he might do to be more respectful. You end the conversation on a positive, encouraging note.

What is very interesting about using and enforcing collective commitments is they keep the conversation impersonal. The conversation with Ray was not personal. Ray did not violate your rule or value; he violated a commitment, a promise, that he made with every member of the teaching staff. He knows word will spread and this will be embarrassing. You are hopeful that Ray will keep his emotions in check when similar situations arise. The staff will know you are holding everyone accountable for their commitments and for their behavior.

A benefit of this process is the lens is positive, not negative. Instead of looking for misbehaviors and violations of the values, you learn to look for individuals and teams that are doing what everyone on campus committed to doing. What an incredible cultural tool!

Looking through the lens of the collective commitments does not have to be exclusive to the principalship. The guiding coalition can also recognize and celebrate teams and individuals who exemplify the school's values. The guiding coalition could create a process whereby members identify any member of the staff (including support staff) who lives the school's values (much like Candice was recognized for treating others with respect in the preceding example). Staff members can be on any team, department, or grade level.

For example, when a member of the guiding coalition witnesses another staff member or a team living and modeling a specific collective commitment, he or she could notify the principal about what was observed. The principal would then generate a brief note to that staff member or team about how much they are appreciated for modeling one of the school's values. Schools that enculturate the process of breathing life into the collective commitments can elevate trust and collaboration to higher degrees than ever before.

Voices From the Field

My advice to principals about creating and leading guiding coalitions is this.

1. Get very, very clear on your focus and your norms.

2. Support members in developing the skills to facilitate crucial conversations with peers.

3. Provide deep and ongoing support and professional development to members to ensure that they understand the why behind the work and decisions.

4. Don't hesitate to make a change when you have members who, with support, feedback, and professional development, don't live up to their commitments.

—K–8 District Superintendent, Illinois

Goals

The fourth pillar requires that PLCs set goals to identify priorities along with their targets and timelines. PLC goals answer the question, "What goals will we use to monitor our progress?" An easy way to create goals and monitor progress is through the process of setting SMART goals. *SMART* is an acronym for strategic and specific, measurable, attainable, results oriented, and time bound (Conzemius & O'Neill, 2014). Figure 3.8 features the SMART goal worksheet, which can assist your guiding coalition in determining and developing SMART goals for the school. Since the guiding coalition does not develop the goals of individual collaborative teams, they, too, may use the SMART goal worksheet to determine and develop their team-level goals.

SMART Goal Worksheet				
School: **Team Name:** **Team Leader:** **Team Members:** **District Goal(s):** **School Goal(s):**				
Team SMART Goal	Strategies and Action Steps	Who Is Responsible	Target Date or Timeline	Evidence of Effectiveness

Source: DuFour et al., 2016, p. 101.

FIGURE 3.8: SMART goal worksheet.

*Visit **go.SolutionTree.com/PLCbooks** for a free reproducible version of this figure.*

Conclusion

You would never intentionally build a home for you and your family on a weak, improperly laid foundation. You would never allow shortcuts or poor-quality materials. You would never approve of processes or decisions that are potentially harmful. Oddly enough, there are those of us who, as careful and cautious as we are for our own families, allow shortcuts to the PLC process. Leaders need to ensure they do not fall victim to these damaging practices.

Building the foundation for your PLC is a critical part of the PLC process because it sets the tone for future work, communication, trust, and relationships. If you take shortcuts or make omissions when building the foundation, your PLC will suffer. It is far better to take the time to build the foundation properly the first time than it is to rush through the process or skip an important piece only to go back and shore things up later with temporary or insufficient patches. Time saved by shortcuts will be lost when correcting the damage.

The primary connections between the PLC school structure and the students you serve are the personnel you lead. Chapter 4 focuses on establishing and strengthening the interactions that you and your guiding coalition will depend on to create a strong, positive PLC culture.

▶ Next Steps

The next steps toward ensuring a strong PLC culture will be to assess where your school currently is with regard to the five initial actions, or footings, to creating a PLC.

With your guiding coalition, review the process for setting your PLC footings and complete the assessment tool in figure 3.9 (page 82). Use this tool to determine what is going well in your journey toward becoming a PLC and to identify opportunities for improvement. Can you identify which footings are strong and help support a positive culture? Do parts of the process need attention? If so, which areas need attention; and what actions need to be taken to ensure the footings are properly in place?

Complete the same process to assess your four pillars. Share the assessment with your guiding coalition. What can your team celebrate? What work needs to be done to bring your foundation up to "building code"?

? FAQs

This is my first year as principal. Our school's mission statement was created a couple of years ago by the administrators. They included no staff input or agreement in the process or the outcome. How do we make the mission creation process more inclusive to ensure owner-ship as we move forward? How can I lead the change without making it look like I'm simply trying to undo another team's work?

Initial Steps to Ensuring a Strong PLC Culture	What has been done to embed this step into the PLC culture?	What evidence do you have that your efforts have been effective?	Are there weak or ineffective aspects of this step that need to be strengthened? If so, what are they and what actions can you take?
Build shared knowledge of PLC characteristics and their links to the research of effective schooling practices.			
Build shared knowledge of the current reality in your district or school.			
Develop a guiding coalition.			
Establish a common vocabulary.			
Celebrate your progress on the PLC journey.			

Source: Adapted from Keating et al., 2008.

FIGURE 3.9: Tool for assessing the initial stages to ensuring a strong PLC culture.

Visit **go.SolutionTree.com/PLCbooks** for a free reproducible version of this figure.

Begin by sharing the situation with your guiding coalition members to get their input and ideas. You might ask, "How can we honor the work of the team that started the PLC process and build on its work to move to the next level?" What the previous team did was not right or wrong. It did the work with good intentions and helped point the school in the correct direction.

After learning the importance of creating a mission statement that all staff members can support, your guiding coalition will find it easier to recommend the change to create a new mission statement that can instill pride and motivate everyone. When the staff understand the new mission statement would better serve the school's needs, there will unlikely be hurt feelings or negative attitudes toward the new work. The guiding coalition's input and comments will help you lead the change. To ensure that it does not look like you are the one changing everything, consider letting the guiding coalition members lead the mission-development process. Your staff will tend to trust their judgment and leadership.

Our district requires that our schools use the district's mission and vision statements rather than create unique statements for each school. We recognize the importance of each school's creating its statements, but the district mandate takes precedence. What can we do?

The answer depends on your leadership, your relationship with the district leaders, and the politics of your district. In some situations, school leaders might have relationships with district staff and a level of experience and credibility that might allow them to convince district leaders that individualized foundational materials for schools are a good idea. In others, school leaders would not even entertain the thought of going against the district mandate. If you do work in a district that requires uniformity, it's not worth falling on that sword. Support the idea openly and privately. Chances are the statements are written in general-enough terms that your guiding coalition will be able to make them applicable to your school. If the district demands that all schools use the district's mission and vision but allows them to create their collective commitments and goals, you'll be in good shape. Your teams will be able to create school-specific collective commitments and goals that can easily align with the district's mission and vision.

Quite frankly, I believe all this mission and vision creation is a waste of time. It's unnecessary fluff. Shouldn't we be spending time and resources on the real work of PLCs, common formative assessments, response to intervention, and so on?

This is not an uncommon question, especially if you and your school have had negative experiences with the processes. Perhaps these foundational elements were handed down from on high or rushed so that the ideas didn't stick with your staff. There are many possibilities as to why you believe the pillars of a PLC are fluff. I recommend that you give creating a PLC foundation another chance before you quit altogether. If the research did not overwhelmingly show that the foundational elements are essential, and if the PLC at Work architects did not believe these pieces were important, the PLC process would omit them. Your staff need a rallying cry, a central focus, a common ground they all can put their foot on and say, "This is what we believe. This is what inspires us to work together for the benefit of all our students!"

Sports teams at all levels, corporations, and businesses large and small spend billions each year on branding and on selling a lifestyle or way of doing something that makes you want to be part of it. They set a direction and paint a picture that people can relate to and feel motivated by. If it's important enough for businesses, industries, and so on, then it is certainly part of the PLC process that you will want to include. Your school, your home, and the businesses you frequent have foundations without exception. Wouldn't it make sense for your PLC to have one as well?

I am not very creative. I believe in the power of mission and vision, but I seem unable to inspire my staff with them. Currently, the mission and vision are just two laminated documents on the walls of the school. How do I make them motivational, inspirational, and real?

Chances are excellent that there are teachers, support personnel, and perhaps even students who can help you be inspirational. Another untapped resource might be business leaders in your community who frequently work with mission- and vision-related activities. You and your guiding coalition might consider pulling some of them together and presenting your challenge for their discussion and perspective. You may find having these business leaders look at your challenge from a completely different angle, a noneducational angle, most helpful. How do they use their missions? How do they inspire with vision? What do they do to keep their organizations grounded in the organizations' values and principles?

We have one team that simply does not want to change. The team members like the school the way it is. They seem to think there is nothing wrong with the traditional school structure. Even their colleague who is on the guiding coalition is reluctant to lead his team to collaborate. How do I handle this?

You may wish to refer to the section in this chapter on building the PLC footings (page 63). Make sure that the staff have what information they need on the research behind effective collaborative practices. Provide student achievement data and other information that compares your teams with similar teams across the district, state, or province. Especially share data from high-performing PLCs that serve similar populations. What are those teams doing that your resistant team can do to get similar results? Why are this team's members so resistant? Do they need more information? Do they not believe their students can learn at higher levels? What ideas and suggestions can your guiding coalition offer the leader of this team? Have your guiding coalition members shared best practices with the team leader, along with how their teams overcame similar challenges of making the change? However you deal with this challenge throughout the current year, your administrative team will want to start planning to change this team's makeup next year even if it involves moving personnel or bringing new personnel on board.

◤ Reflection

Reflect on the foundation and structure (specifically, the PLC footings and pillars) of your school. What are three specific areas that, if you and your guiding coalition prioritized them, would make a significant and positive difference in your school? What high-leverage, high-impact actions can you and your team take now that will help strengthen your PLC footings or foundation? Once you've taken those actions, list the results you observed and ideas for how you can continue to improve on the three areas. Use the "Action Plan for Improving Your PLC Foundation or Structure" to record your thoughts, make plans for next steps, and monitor your progress.

Action Plan for Improving Your PLC Foundation or Structure

Areas of Focus to Improve Your PLC Foundation or Structure	High-Leverage, High-Impact Actions to Take	Results of Your Actions	Additional Actions to Take as a Result of the Improvements You Have Made

CHAPTER 4

BUILDING POWERFUL RELATIONSHIPS

The fundamental pillars of school leadership are relationships; nothing substitutes for building and nurturing them.

—Joanne Rooney

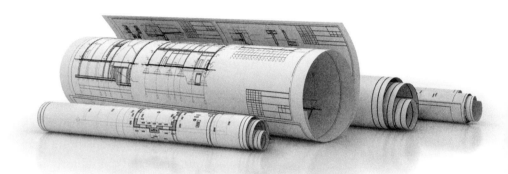

Think for a moment of what happens when you touch the still surface of a body of water: ripples move out from the center in a circular pattern. Leadership affects stakeholders in much the same way; as a leader, you create a ripple effect that spreads exponentially through the relationships you develop and nurture with your guiding coalition. The ripples then continue to move out through your school and beyond. Many aspects of leadership impact the quality of the ripples you produce. Are there gaps? Spots with still water? Building powerful relationships with the members of your guiding coalition and the rest of your school will help you create the perfect circular pattern to support PLC transformation and effectively address the barriers to organizational change.

Lead More, Manage Less

School leadership involves both leading and managing. Leadership and management are not in competition with each other: "Leadership complements management; it doesn't replace it" (Kotter, 1999, p. 52). As Timothy Kanold (2011) notes, management's primary focus is not people, but leadership's focus is; however, strong leadership without management can result in chaos, and strong management without leadership creates excessively bureaucratic schools where engagement is minimal and accountability for implementation is practically absent. So building powerful relationships requires school leaders to embrace both positions—those of manager and leader of individuals in their guiding coalition and collaborative teams.

John Kotter (1999) defines leadership "as the development of vision and strategies, the alignment of relevant people behind those strategies, and the empowerment of individuals to make the vision happen, despite obstacles" (p. 10). He contrasts the meaning of management as "keeping the current system operating through planning, budgeting, organizing, staffing, controlling, and problem solving" (Kotter, 1999, p. 10). He concludes his comparison by describing leadership as "soft and hot" and working "through people and culture" and management as "harder and cooler" and working "through hierarchy and systems" (Kotter, 1999, p. 10).

There is no hard and fast rule on what percentage of your time should be spent leading your PLC efforts compared to what percentage should be spent managing resources to support your PLC. The lines between the two are blurred. The ratio of management to leadership in most organizations is around 80:20 (Jackson, 2020). Fortune 50 CEOs might spend 70% of their time leading, 20% managing, and 10% coaching (Winter, 2017). You should not get caught up in worrying about how much time is spent leading, managing, coaching, mentoring, reading, and so on. When finding a balance that works for you and your PLC, what matters most is that you increase your focus on leadership behaviors, responsibilities, and actions more than it currently is. Become more aware of how you spend your time, and consciously invest more of it leading than managing.

Management responsibilities and actions are required to strengthen and enhance your leadership style. You cannot lead without them. However, they should only serve in a supportive role and not dominate your attention or your schedule. You will find that focusing more on followers and their needs (leadership) and less on things and subordinates (management) will help build and improve your relationships. Significant organizational and cultural change can only be led. It cannot be mandated. Change that is forced and not driven by vision and mission can only result in temporary trans-formation, window dressing. Temporary change eventually fades over time because it has not been deeply embedded into the culture of the school.

Powerful guiding coalitions can make necessary changes in their schools despite forces that impede or challenge the initiative (Kotter, 1996). Powerful relationships bound by trust and a common goal fuel powerful guiding coalitions. In his landmark work on overcoming the barriers to organizational change, John Kotter (1996) does not advocate types of power where the leader exerts power over subordinates. Kotter's (1996) work centers on the business world, but these types of power exist in schools as well. For PLCs to operate at their optimum, such power structures should reside quietly in the background to give way to the more indirect and understated power found through collaboration. Power in collaborative processes comes from the combined work of teams and is abundantly available for all to share and benefit from. Power that results in control over others flows from a scarcity mentality, where only so much power is available and only a precious few can have it—usually those with power of position and title. This thinking runs counter to the work of true PLCs.

Model Strong Relationships

How you treat, communicate with, and relate to others on the guiding coalition and on your staff will set the tone for relationships in your school. Likewise, the relationships among your guiding coalition members provide the critical foundation for the rest of the staff. Members of the guiding coalition model collaboration and other PLC behaviors for the members of their collaborative teacher teams. A first step in modeling strong relationships in your guiding coalition is to develop team norms that show expectations for both the school leader and guiding coalition members. On a regular basis, assess how well your behaviors and interactions with team members reflect these norms.

The following list includes sample team norms that support powerful relationships among your teams. Your list of norms will not be as extensive. It might only include the four to six norms that best meet your teams' specific operational needs.

- We're all colleagues; we respect each other.

- Everyone participates; no one person dominates.

- We honor time limits. We arrive on time. We begin on time. We return from breaks on time. We end on time.

- We listen to our colleagues as allies. We listen empathically.

- It's OK to disagree. It's not OK to be disagreeable.

- We represent a common interest. No one represents a special interest.

- Students' educational needs come first.

- We respect confidentiality.

- All input is valid and accepted.

- We value diversity among our team members, and we celebrate differences.

- No question is ever considered dumb.

- We maintain focus on the content and processes of our guiding coalition meetings and sessions.

- When appropriate, we have fun and bring joy to our guiding coalition meetings. We strive to make our meetings and tasks the kind of work that we look forward to.

- We focus on behaviors, not personalities. We use our team-developed and team-approved accountability protocols to address violation of any team norms.

One method for determining your team norms is for members of your teams to answer the following question: "In meetings that you have experienced, what are some behaviors that have gotten in the way of holding a successful meeting or that have gotten your meeting off track? Identify those behaviors, but do not identify the specific meeting or individuals by name." List the behaviors or actions on chart paper. Sample responses might include people coming to the meeting late, people who come to the meeting unprepared, talk that is off-topic, sidebar conversations, and so on.

After all input and suggestions are listed, have your team write the negative behaviors and actions as norms. For example, the norm to address people coming to the meeting late might be written as, "We will honor time limits." The norm to address people coming to the meeting unprepared could be, "We will come to our meetings prepared." The norm to address sidebar conversations might be, "During discussions, one person speaks at a time." To address off-topic talk, the norm might be, "We will maintain focus." Once your list of suggested norms is developed, the team must agree to them.

The team-developed, team-approved norms are referred to during the meeting, and violations are addressed by the team, not the leader or a sergeant at arms. Teams are mutually accountable for their actions and behaviors and must collectively enforce their norms.

Figure 4.1 will assist you and your guiding coalition members in reflecting on relationships within the guiding coalition and within their collaborative teams. This tool can be used as an individual reflection tool or as a team reflection tool.

Creating a powerful guiding coalition involves emphasizing and nurturing powerful relationships. Powerful relationships might best be described as those that can endure despite being broadsided by conflict, disagreement, negativity, and disappointment. Several important characteristics, principles, and values go into creating powerful relationships. They might include:

- Vulnerability—"The quality or state of having little resistance to some outside agent" (Vulnerability, n.d.)

- Flexibility—"Being readily capable to adapt to new, different, or changing requirements" (Flexibility, n.d.)

- Respect—"An attitude of consideration or high regard" (Respect, n.d.)

- Trust—"Assured reliance on the character, ability, strength, or truth of someone or something" (Trust, n.d.)

Expected Behaviors of Guiding Coalition Members	How Is Our Guiding Coalition Doing?	How Am I Doing?	Actions Required
We're all colleagues; we respect each other.			
Everyone participates; no one person dominates.			
We honor time limits: We arrive on time. We begin on time. We return from breaks on time. We end on time.			
We listen to our colleagues as allies. We listen empathically.			
It's OK to disagree. It's not OK to be disagreeable.			
We represent a common interest. No one represents a special interest.			
Students' educational needs come first.			
We respect confidentiality.			
All input is valid and accepted.			
We value diversity among our team members, and we celebrate differences.			

FIGURE 4.1: Relationship self-assessment for guiding coalition members.   continued →

Expected Behaviors of Guiding Coalition Members	How Is Our Guiding Coalition Doing?	How Am I Doing?	Actions Required
No question is ever considered dumb.			
We maintain focus on the content and processes of our guiding coalition meetings and sessions.			
When appropriate, we have fun and bring joy to our guiding coalition meetings. We strive to make our meetings and tasks the kind of work that we look forward to.			
We focus on behaviors, not personalities. We use our team-developed and team-approved accountability protocols to address violation of any team norms.			

Visit **go.SolutionTree.com/PLCbooks** *for a free reproducible version of this figure.*

- Commitment—"A promise, vow, or agreement to do something" (Commitment, n.d.)

- Honesty—"Being truthful in what you say and in what you do" (Honesty, n.d.)

- Transparency—"Clarity and openness in actions" (Transparency, n.d.)

When principals initially concentrate their efforts to establish and cultivate these characteristics, the resulting beliefs, attitudes, and behaviors can enhance the guiding coalition's effectiveness and power. The principal cannot be a bystander in the relationship-building, relationship-strengthening process. The principal has to be an active participant in the process by understanding the importance of relationships and how to develop and nurture them. These relationships are fundamental to the effective execution of many other responsibilities of school leaders.

Build Trust

Mike Mattos, Richard DuFour, Rebecca DuFour, Robert Eaker, and Thomas W. Many (2016) clarify how school leaders go about building trust.

> Principals set the tone for building high-trust relationships in their schools, but they cannot accomplish the task alone. Principals and teachers alike share responsibility for building trust. The key component of trust is aligning one's behaviors with one's words, having the outlook of "We do what we say we will do." This is why establishing and honoring collective commitments is so vital to the PLC process. The single best strategy for creating a trusting environment is clarifying how members will behave and then acting accordingly. (p. 69)

Austin Buffum (2008) has called trust the secret ingredient to successful shared leadership. Scholars and authors Warren Bennis and Burt Nanus (2007) define trust as "the emotional glue that binds followers and leaders together . . . the basic ingredient of all organizations, the lubrication that makes it possible for organizations to work" (p. 41). To build and maintain trust, school leaders are to be aware of potential barriers they may encounter that can derail or destroy trust. Obstacles or threats to trust among guiding coalition members might include top-down decision making, which they can view as autocratic, misleading, or not in keeping with the school's best interest; poor communication; inconsistent or inadequate follow-through; and frequent turnover of administrative personnel or leadership team members.

"School leaders need to see trust as the bridge that PLC reform must travel across, and that bridge is built incrementally through carefully made decisions and constant modeling by the leader" (Buffum, 2008, p. 69). It is through the principal's leadership of the guiding coalition that the modeled behavior is spread throughout the school.

In her book *Trust Matters: Leadership for Successful Schools*, Megan Tschannen-Moran (2014) identifies five key elements of trust. Trust is "one's willingness to be vulnerable to another based on the confidence that the other is benevolent, honest, open, reliable, and competent" (Tschannen-Moran, 2014, pp. 19–20). These five key ingredients that Tschannen-Moran (2014) shares (benevolence, honesty, openness, reliability, and competence) create trustworthy leadership. Principals who focus on these five facets will strengthen the levels of trust they have with their guiding coalitions. The stronger the trust they have, the more powerful their teams can become. Table 4.1 (page 94) lists Tschannen-Moran's five facets of trust with a brief explanation of each.

Table 4.1: The Five Facets of Trust

Facet of Trust	Description
Benevolence	School leaders can promote trust by demonstrating benevolence: showing consideration and sensitivity for employees' needs and interests, acting in a way that protects employees' rights, and refraining from exploiting others for personal gain.
Honesty	Honesty concerns a person's character, integrity, and authenticity. Integrity is the perceived match between a person's values as expressed in words and those expressed through actions. Authenticity means the willingness to accept responsibility not just for the good things that happen but for the mistakes and negative outcomes as well.
Openness	Openness is a process by which people make themselves vulnerable to others by sharing information, influence, and control. It means the disclosure of facts, alternatives, intentions, judgments, and feelings.
Reliability	A definition of reliability is when one can depend on another consistently. Reliability combines a sense of predictability with caring and competence.
Competence	Competence is the ability to perform a task as expected, according to appropriate standards. Skills related to competence include setting high standards, pressing for results, solving problems, resolving conflict, working hard, and setting an example.

Source: Tschannen-Moran, 2014, pp. 33–39.

The Be, Do, Have Model for Building Trust

One way to reflect on how powerful trust is in your relationships is to apply Tschannen-Moran's (2014) five facets of trust through a simple yet potentially powerful coaching tool: the Be, Do, Have model, represented in figure 4.2.

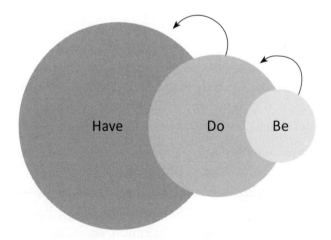

FIGURE 4.2: Be, Do, Have model.

If your goal is to become more powerful by increasing your level of trust, you can approach your goal in one of three different ways: (1) as a victim, (2) as a worker, or (3) as a winner (Frazer, 2018). Only one of them works.

The first approach (Frazer, 2018), have, do, be, is used by victims. This approach puts have at the center of their circle. The victim's focus is to attain things they currently do not have so their desire to have drives everything. The victim tells himself or herself,

"When I have time to strengthen my relationships, I will do more shared decision making with my guiding coalition. Then I'll be seen as a more open leader. The dilemma is I don't have that time yet. I don't make time to involve others in decisions because I can make more decisions quicker than if I involved others. If I only had the time the principal down the road dedicates to decision making, I'd be seen as having the same openness as she has in her relationships. But I don't have the time, so I'm not as open as I want to be." Victims wait for outside conditions to change before they can move forward in their work. They become victims of their desire to attain something they do not have.

The next approach to achieving goals is that of the worker. The worker seeks goals in this order: do, have, be. The center of the worker's circle is doing. The worker's thinking is the more that is done, the happier or more successful they will become. The worker says, "The more I do to strengthen my shared decision making with my guiding coalition, the more vulnerability I'll have. The more vulnerability I have, the more successful I'll be. The problem with do, have, be is the more I do, the more there is to be done. I am defined by what I do, so I become driven, busy, and exhausted. When I have more, I then have more to lose. That fear causes me to work even harder. My work is do, do, do. There seems to be no letup." A myth exists that the more you have, the happier or more successful you will become. In reality, the more you have, the more you will do to have even more. The cycle seems never-ending.

The last approach is that of the winner who follows the Be, Do, Have model. The center of the winner's model is be. The winner does not begin with the desire or need to have openness in relationships. The winner does not ask, "What must I have before I begin, or what work must I do?" The winner's approach begins with, "What do I need or want to be?" When a winner decides what person he or she wants to become, the winner is ready to answer the question, "To be a more open leader, what would I do?" If the leader decides that to be more open, he or she needs to share or increase decision making with the guiding coalition, then his or her *have* will take care of itself. That principal will have more openness.

The Be, Do, Have approach is an inside-out approach to improving your leadership and relationships because you have the power to change what you have control over. You are in charge of what you can become. Other approaches to personal or leadership change require your control over conditions and resources that may be out of your reach or out of your control.

Actions to Strengthen Trust

Making the leadership of your school more powerful begins with you! You own the characteristics and traits that all great leaders own. You are ready to pass on those characteristics to your guiding coalition. Following the Be, Do, Have paradigm gives you and your team the best chance to lead in powerful ways. *Be* the leader who can *do* whatever it takes to *have* what you and your teams require for the benefit of your students and staff!

Table 4.2 (page 96) provides suggested actions and behaviors that principals might consider to strengthen or improve the five facets of trust.

Table 4.2: Actions and Behaviors That Strengthen Trust

What Must I *Be?*	What Must I *Do?*	So That I Can *Have . . .*
Benevolent	Care, extend goodwill, demonstrate positive intentions, support teachers, express appreciation for faculty and staff efforts, be fair, guard confidential information	Benevolence: Caring relationships and the best interest of others at heart
Honest	Show integrity, tell the truth, keep promises, honor agreements, be authentic, accept responsibility, avoid manipulation, be real, be true to myself	Honesty: Relationships based on authenticity and integrity
Open	Maintain open communication, share important information, delegate, share decision making, share power	Openness: Relationships where "I make myself vulnerable to others by sharing information, influence, and control" (Tschannen-Moran, 2014, p. 28)
Reliable	Be consistent, be dependable, show commitment, express dedication, exercise diligence	Reliability: Predictability in my relationships to "do what is expected on a regular and consistent basis" (Tschannen-Moran, 2014, p. 33)
Competent	Buffer teachers from outside disruptions, handle difficult situations, set standards, press for results, work hard, set an example, solve problems, resolve conflict, be flexible	Competence: The "ability to perform tasks as expected according to appropriate standards" (Tschannen-Moran, 2014, p. 35)

Austin Buffum (2008) outlines additional actions and behaviors that can strengthen and enhance trust among team members. Use figure 4.3 to assist your guiding coalition to reflect on these suggestions and to determine which actions and behaviors are present among your team and which you can improve.

Actions to Repair Broken Trust

There will be times when trust between individuals or teams will be broken or violated. When those instances occur, they cannot be ignored or overlooked. When feelings or emotions that arise from a broken trust are neglected or buried, they can appear later in uglier ways (Covey, 1989). Since trust is an essential part of creating *powerful* guiding coalitions, it must be brought front and center as an agenda item during your guiding coalition meetings. You do not have the luxury to hope that incidents of broken trust will heal on their own; hope is not a sound leadership strategy. Trust must be a topic that the guiding coalition purposefully addresses on a consistent basis because of the dynamic nature of the changing relationships on your staff.

A solid, trusting relationship that you have had with an individual or team for years can suddenly be in jeopardy because of a violation of trust. For example, trust is violated if you promise a collaborative team equipment or resources but do not deliver, creating a rift in your relationship. Another example is if you share with another person something a staff member told you in absolute confidence (Tschannen-Moran, 2014). When unfulfilled promises, broken confidentiality, and other types of betrayal occur, you must address them and attempt to repair the damage.

Actions and Behaviors That Strengthen and Enhance Trust Among Members of the Guiding Coalition	How Is Our Guiding Coalition Doing in This Area?	If This Action or Behavior Needs to Be Strengthened, What Can Our Guiding Coalition Do to Strengthen or Improve in This Area?
Create and monitor team-developed, team-approved values (collective commitments). Use team-developed, team-approved accountability protocols to deal with violations to the values.		
Operate with honesty and integrity.		
Be available.		
Demonstrate a caring attitude.		
Listen.		
Encourage risk taking.		
Share decision making.		
Value dissent.		
Don't be consumed by accountability.		
Make sure members have what they need to lead.		
Be prepared to confront ineffectiveness.		
Make relationships a priority.		
Promote relationship building through professional learning.		
Involve staff in discussions that focus on the school's mission, vision, values, and goals.		
Create frequent meaningful opportunities for team members to work together collaboratively.		

Source: Adapted from Buffum, 2008.

FIGURE 4.3: Actions and behaviors that strengthen and enhance trust among collaborative teams.

*Visit **go.SolutionTree.com/PLCbooks** for a free reproducible version of this figure.*

Susan Stephenson (2009), author of *Leading With Trust*, outlines a few key points to consider when trying to repair a violation of trust:

- If the incident was public, more people may need to be involved in the solution.

- It matters whether the incident was inadvertent or intentional.

- An apology or atonement is the most difficult step in repairing trust.

- Apologies are always a good thing.

- Sincerity is a factor, as well as timing.

- It is more difficult to rebuild trust once it is damaged in a mature relationship.

- Trust repair is a bilateral process. (p. 20)

Empower Others

A PLC is a collaborative culture in which leadership is shared by all staff members regardless of years of experience, position, expertise, and so on. In a PLC, "all means all" should apply to students (all students can learn at high levels) and teachers, administrators, and staff alike. The education profession is not a spectator sport where some colleagues are out on the field getting muddy and sweaty while the rest of the staff are in the stands watching, cheering, and eating popcorn. *All* really does mean *all!*

In addition, leaders who attempt to do everything for everybody all the time without empowering others to succeed and lead often face burnout. The solution to leading effectively and wisely is by leveraging your leadership through those you lead—developing capacity for all to be leaders. The collaborative culture of a PLC requires leaders to empower staff members to work toward achieving the mission, vision, collective commitments, and goals of the school. A workplace that supports, creates, and promotes opportunities for empowerment can be powerful in terms of impact and professionalism.

There are many schools of thought on what empowerment is and how it can affect employees. Some sources define empowerment as "the loss of control" (BrainMass, n.d.); "delegating authority and decision-making, sharing information, and asking for . . . input" (Lee, Willis, & Tian, 2018); or "the granting of the power, right, or authority to perform various acts or duties" (Empowerment, n.d.).

In *Trust in Schools: A Core Resource for Improvement*, Anthony Bryk and Barbara Schneider (2002) outline four criteria that, when combined, create empowerment: (1) respect, (2) competence, (3) personal regard for others, and (4) integrity. Empowerment creates cultures based on shared learning, shared leadership, and continuous school improvement (Erkens & Twadell, 2012). Effective PLC leaders create opportunities for creativity and empowerment; they do not hurl directives that disempower staff and allow blame and criticism to creep in.

Patrick Bosworth (n.d.), founder and CEO of Leadership Choice, states that leaders should consider putting the following eight elements in place to create a more empowering culture.

1. Delegate for individual growth and development.

2. Establish specific expectations for the outcomes.

3. Give staff freedom over how they complete tasks or assignments.

4. Offer resources, tools, and support necessary to accomplish the work.

5. Provide specific and meaningful feedback.

6. Be receptive to the staff's points of view and suggestions.

7. Connect their work back to the vision of the school.

8. Show appreciation for their contributions.

Roland S. Barth (2001) suggests school leaders can develop and increase leadership when they encourage teachers to participate in problem solving and decision making before the final solution is reached—not afterward. The following sections offer some examples of how to put these elements into action among your guiding coalition members to empower them.

Assuming Meeting Responsibilities

You may give teacher leaders, as members of your guiding coalition, limited opportunities for empowering experiences during meetings. For example, you might ask a guiding coalition member to plan, organize, and facilitate a meeting by preparing the agenda, communicating details of the meeting with the guiding coalition, preparing the meeting room and materials, and conducting the session. The two of you may meet to discuss the purpose of the meeting along with the desired outcomes. You would answer any questions the team member might have and let him or her know you are available at any time for assistance. Afterward, meet with the team member to debrief the session, give feedback, and recognize his or her efforts and the positive results of the meeting.

Creating Values (Collective Commitments)

Another example of an empowering experience is to give two guiding coalition members the responsibility of leading the faculty through the process to create the school's values (collective commitments). After laying out the task and outcomes, they assemble their ad hoc team to plan and conduct the process. As principal, you serve as an available resource, but you do not directly lead or involve yourself unless necessary.

Leading Grade-Level or Department Teams

Leading the grade-level or department-level teams during their collaborative team times can empower guiding coalition members. These are the times when the guiding coalition members are on their own to lead their teams through the collaborative team processes. During these team meetings, guiding coalition members in turn pass on empowering opportunities to the teacher level. Collaborative team leaders can organize their individual teams by assigning roles (or asking for volunteers) during the collaborative team time. Assigning roles such as *facilitator*, *recorder*, and even *participant*, describes the specific responsibilities that each member will have during the team meetings. When all team members have roles to fulfill, they tend to be more engaged and committed to the work of the team.

During collaborative team meetings, tasks, responsibilities, and so forth should be assigned to individual team members for completion before the next meeting. Working on these responsibilities and tasks gives team members great opportunities to apply their leadership skills and training to their work. When empowered to add to the quality of a team's work, team members can enjoy the satisfaction of accomplishment and contribution to the team effort. Time during guiding coalition meetings might be given to team members to share how well their team members are doing with their roles and responsibilities.

Building in Safety Measures

Anytime you are leading others to take risks or stretch their leadership muscles, you will want to build in safety measures to ensure they are successful. You would not give them their charge and allow them to flounder, struggle, and fail. You should build in a mechanism to intervene if you see the project going sideways. Depending on the complexity of the task, you might schedule regular times to touch base and check in to see what questions there are or what support or resources the team member needs. These established intervention times give your team members guardrails to keep their work going in the right direction and keep them from going over the edge.

Voices From the Field

As I lead, I lead with gentle pressure relentlessly applied.
—Secondary School Principal, Canada

An empowering work environment is essential to ensure continuous improvement and continuous learning in PLCs. When principals build powerful relationships, they can create school cultures that value and encourage the empowerment of teams and team leaders (Marzano, Waters, & McNulty, 2005). Principals can be flexible when they empower teacher leaders to share their collective knowledge through collaboration (Bowgren & Sever, 2010). PLCs can be described as communities of empowerment when they enable and empower teachers to learn and work together for the benefit of all their students (Blankstein, Houston, & Cole, 2008). When guided by their values (collective commitments), administrators and teachers are empowered by their role in shaping a new future for their school (DuFour et al., 2008).

While providing empowering opportunities to individual members of your guiding coalition may be your initial goal, you will want to consider broadening your horizon. PLCs are fueled by teamwork and collaboration; therefore, your ultimate goal is self-directed, self-led collaborative teams through team empowerment.

As a leader, you cannot give people power; and you cannot make those you lead empowered. What you can do, however, is provide others the opportunities, resources, and support they need to become involved themselves. Empowerment becomes a process that develops power in people for use in their own lives; they use this power to act on matters they deem important. When those you lead take steps to improve their own personal and professional lives, they become empowered (Page & Czuba, 1999). The leadership role in the empowerment process becomes one of support, encouragement, and inspiration. As Chinese philosopher Lao Tzu wrote, "When the best leader's work is done the people say, 'We did it ourselves'" (Miller, n.d.).

Seek Information and Awareness and Acknowledge Needs

In *School Leadership That Works*, Robert Marzano, Timothy Waters, and Brian McNulty (2005) note there are several leadership actions or behaviors that can strengthen principal-teacher relationships: "being informed about significant personal issues within the lives of staff members; being aware of personal needs of teachers; acknowledging significant events in the lives of staff members; and maintaining personal relationships with teachers" (p. 59). When principals model these types of behaviors for guiding coalitions, they strengthen relationships among the team members, who then model those behaviors with members of collaborative teams.

One strategy for becoming informed and aware so you can acknowledge needs and establish or improve relationships is to schedule individual meetings with every employee on the staff, from the assistant principal to the half-time cafeteria cashier and everyone in between. If you have a large staff, divide responsibility for personal meetings among your administrative team. Although leaders are busy, making time for these meetings is a great investment in enhancing your relationships with staff.

These meetings can be short—from fifteen to twenty minutes long. Do not sit behind your desk; rather, choose an area where there is nothing between you and the staff member. Have with you an empty legal pad and something to write with. State the purpose of the meeting is to learn what is going well and what needs improvement in the school. Ask questions, listen, and write. The first time you do this activity, you will most likely get very little input, and that's OK. Staff members can find it intimidating to meet with their school leaders. They might wonder, "Why is she asking *me* these questions? What is she going to do with *my* responses? Is she going to like what I say or not?"

It is necessary to anticipate their concerns and anxiety, and reassure them that you (or your administrative team) are meeting with every employee to get an overall picture of what is going well at your school and what improvements are needed. One way you might consider starting your conversations is to refer to the school's mission, vision, and values. Remind each employee that he or she is a valued member of the collaborative culture. One of the best ways to improve the culture is to involve everyone and seek their ideas and opinions. Another way to ease their concerns is by acknowledging that you are listening. Open, receptive body language in a welcome, non-threatening environment helps.

Of course, there will be those employees whose relationships with you might be strained or tense. Nonetheless, they are members of your staff just like everyone else. They have ideas and concerns. Sharing them with you might be the first step in legitimizing their concerns and letting them know you do care. Relationship-building activities like this are a way to soften those relationships and improve them over time. Also ask what you can do to support each staff member. Ask if he or she has suggestions for programs, processes, procedures, and so on that you might consider adding, keeping, or dropping. For example, they may ask questions like, "Could the school add age-appropriate playground equipment for the youngest students?"; "Would it be possible for me to shadow a more experienced instructional assistant so that I can get new ideas about how to support my classroom teacher?"; and "Could we consider doing something with all the 'Do not do this and do not do that' signs everywhere around the building? They are not very welcoming and are unsightly." Just listen and write; do not make comments or promises to act. Don't interrupt with comments such as, "Do you know what that would cost!?" Sample responses to their ideas or suggestions might include, "I'll put that one down," "I'm taking all these suggestions to the administrative team for discussion," and "I'll look into it."

After gathering responses from all employees, review the information and assemble it in a format that you can take to your administrative team. (Note: You would only take suggestions or ideas to your guiding coalition that have to do with PLC-related ideas or concerns.) Look for patterns and themes in the input you get from the meetings. What can be taken care of immediately? What are the ideas that are really good, but they will take time and other resources to schedule and handle? What suggestions are not realistic, much too costly, or simply cannot be done due to rules or regulations?

Follow-up to this process is situational. Use your judgment on how to follow up and follow through with staff to update them on actions you have considered, taken, or planned as a result of their ideas. In some cases, you might consider sharing some of the more common or schoolwide responses during a faculty meeting. Since your whole staff is involved, you might want to hold a meeting with everyone. If your staff is too large, perhaps a faculty meeting and a separate support staff meeting will do. You could share something like, "We had several suggestions to look at the signage along the front of the school. To create a more welcoming entrance, we will either be removing many of the signs or modifying their look or placement so that the message to our community is more inviting."

Depending on the number of changes or ideas, you can share them during one session, or share outcomes and results throughout the year. When updating staff as a whole, share the idea, concern, or suggestion, but do not identify individuals or teams.

If you haven't dealt with or implemented ideas, suggestions, or concerns, you must address them differently. Go back to the teams or individuals who submitted the ideas or input to provide reasons and follow up. There might be cases where some suggestions could be taken to a special ad hoc committee or team to see if a solution or resolution can be reached. Having the individual or team with the idea or concern on such a committee may help them better understand the challenges to why their suggestion cannot be implemented or solved.

If you find this process is successful and helps create a more relationship-focused environment, you might consider conducting similar sessions every other year. When you do the same process again, it will surprise you how open staff members are to sharing with you.

There is no substitute for improving and strengthening relationships among your staff like celebrating and recognizing individuals and teams for the great work that they do.

Conclusion

Leading your PLC transformation can be a daunting and complex task. If, however, you focus your leadership on the most critical element—relationships—you can make this complex task more manageable.

The recipe for creating a successful guiding coalition begins with selecting the right staff members with the right qualities and with the shared purpose to transform your school into a high-performing collaborative culture. However, that is only half the recipe—the ingredients. The other half of the recipe is the process to create, develop, and sustain a *powerful* guiding coalition. The secret is now fully revealed. The best way to accomplish this awesome task is to create an atmosphere and culture in which trust and empowerment are readily available and accessible.

Strong PLC cultures depend on healthy relationships among staff. These relationships are critical to the success of your collaborative learning teams. Strong relationships in a PLC begin at the leadership level. The next chapter will give you the opportunity to look at the power of leading through your guiding coalition and the importance of valuing the differences and talents found among members of your staff.

▶ Next Steps

Think about an individual or a team with which you desire to establish or strengthen trust. Refer back to table 4.2 (page 96). Which facet of trust in the left-hand column (What Must I Be?) will you focus on to achieve your desired results in the relationship you identified? Looking at the middle column (What Must I Do?), what specific action or actions will you take to increase trust in that relationship? How will you know if your actions made a difference? What evidence do you have?

❓ FAQs

Trust is such an important part of all we do. I'm just not sure where to begin to establish, build, or improve trust with my team.

In *Leading Change*, John Kotter (1996) suggests that leaders hold carefully planned off-site events. Your administrative team or several key leaders can help plan such a professional learning event or the team-building, trust-building activities. Kotter (1996) adds that there is to be "lots of talk and joint activities" (p. 66). It surely never hurts to have fun during these special events. They are to be casual and focus on your main objective—to create or enhance your relationships with your team.

The idea of empowerment is something I struggle with. Am I not empowering others when I tell them what to do, delegate tasks, or assign responsibilities?

You are not empowering anyone if you are merely giving others a list of things to do or making them responsible for a particular task. Not all delegated tasks are empowering. Empowerment is more of a process of experiencing personal and internal growth than it is of doing what the principal assigns. Staff members may find satisfaction and some sense of accomplishment when completing assigned tasks, but that in itself is not empowerment. You might consider empowerment as creating a work culture that leads to an awakening in those you lead. If the experience of completing a task or assignment aligns or is congruent with the person's desire to improve or grow in that area, he or she would realize empowerment.

I have an interesting challenge that I am sure other principals have had. I am relatively new to my school, having been here only a couple of years. I have one particular teacher on the guiding coalition who is not a fan of mine. She is a solid team member, very competent. She adored, loved, and worshipped the previous principal, who retired. In fact, they were personal friends whose families socialized outside of school. My challenge is to win her over or at least make our relationship work. I cannot take the place of the previous principal; but surely, I can improve our relationship.

That's a tough one! Since your main focus and desire are to improve your relationship with this teacher, you may consider appealing to something personal and important. Another principal had the same experience. He tried everything to thaw the relationship, but nothing made a difference. Finally, it dawned on him to try to appeal to her strength—being a great mom. During the teacher's annual evaluation conference, the principal commented that all the students in her class were incredibly lucky to have her as their teacher. Why? Just look at how her children turned out—an attorney, a state government employee, and a pastor. All successful. All products of the school system. She walked the walk and talked the talk, and all her students benefited from having her as their teacher. From that moment on, the principal's relationship with the teacher strengthened. Being sincere, appealing to something important, and speaking from the heart made all the difference.

Many of my principal colleagues and I seem to share the same concerns about managing time—especially when it is related to balancing the ratio between leadership and management. Is there a creative way to look at how to tip the balance of leadership and management responsibilities so that we are more proactive and in control as leaders?

Like the majority of school leaders, your challenge is to become more of a leader of learning and less of a victim of schedules, emails, budgeting, reports, and so on. As a PLC leader, you may want to consider changing how you view your school. Do you see your school as two separate structures with an instructional side and a separate support side? If so, do you operate the two sides differently? Are you predominately leading the instructional side and managing the support side?

A paradigm shift you might consider to help increase your time leading and reduce the time managing would be to create an emphasis on leading both the instructional and support services of your school collaboratively. Instead of working collaboratively with your guiding coalition and teacher teams and in isolation to complete your non-instructional duties and responsibilities, consider working differently on how you accomplish the more time-consuming administrative, managerial tasks. If leading the learning through collaboration is your top priority, wouldn't it be more effective to collaboratively lead your more managerial responsibilities as well (for example, custodial services, food services, operational services, budgeting, scheduling, and so on)? You might increase your time to lead by reducing the time working alone handling the more managerial responsibilities of the school. Perhaps implementing more collaborative practices and processes in the way you manage will improve your ratio of leading to managing. Might there be ways to collaboratively lead with your support service personnel in the same way you lead your instructional teams?

Reflection

Think about your relationships with individual staff members or with teams where trust needs to be repaired. After reflecting on the details of these relationships and on how trust was violated, complete the "Action Plan for Repairing a Violation of Trust" (page 106).

Action Plan for Repairing a Violation of Trust

What relationship is in need of repaired trust?	How was trust violated?	In this situation, which of Stephenson's (2009) key points (page 98) will you consider trying?	What actions did you take?	What were the results of your actions?

CHAPTER 5

PROMOTING COLLABORATIVE LEADERSHIP

The strength of the team is each individual member. The strength of each member is the team.

—Phil Jackson

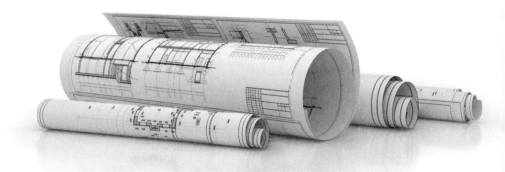

When addressing his junior officers, General Dwight D. Eisenhower demonstrated his philosophy of leadership using string. He would put a small piece of string on each officer's desk and instruct the officers to push their strings. As they pushed, their strings would bunch up on their desktops. General Eisenhower would then tell the officers to pull the strings. As they did, the pieces of string would move easily over the tops of their desks. It did not matter the speed of the pulling, the distance of the pulling, the length of the strings, the sharpness of the turns, or who pulled the strings—the strings faithfully followed when and where they were pulled for as long as they were pulled (Miller, 2008).

In his simple leadership lesson, General Eisenhower was making the point that leaders can be more effective when they lead, or pull, subordinates and teams from the front. Forcing personnel and teams you lead through pushing can result in frustration, anger, resistance, and sabotage. Leaders can pull by being encouraging, by providing resources and professional learning, or by supporting the efforts of others. A guiding coalition that collectively pulls as a team exhibits what is described as collaborative leadership.

PLC school leaders must try to find that delicate balance of leadership that helps keep a steady hand on the keel. Leadership is never one size fits all. As psychologist Abraham Maslow (1966) cautions, "I suppose it is tempting, if the only tool you have is a hammer, to treat everything as if it were a nail" (p. 15). In PLCs, not only does one leadership size not work for every stakeholder, but it is unrealistic to expect one leader to lead everyone all the time for everything. If PLCs do not expect one teacher to know everything about every subject so every student can succeed, then schools cannot depend on a lone leader's leadership in every situation in a collaborative culture.

The way to multiply the lone leader's capacity to lead is through effective collaborative leadership by the guiding coalition.

Collaborative Versus Lone Leadership

Leading through a guiding coalition instead of a lone leader has many benefits. Table 5.1 shows the benefits of leading through a guiding coalition rather than leading the PLC process by yourself.

Table 5.1: Leading Through a Guiding Coalition Versus Leading by Yourself

Collaborative Leadership Through a Guiding Coalition	Leadership by a Lone Leader
Leadership is leveraged; the team shoulders the responsibility, so there is less weight for an individual leader to carry.	This leadership takes an enormous amount of energy. One person shoulders all the leadership weight; leadership is not shared or leveraged.
Multiple leaders offer and consider multiple perspectives.	A single perspective limits options and ideas.
Responsibilities can rotate among team members; when one team member is unavailable, another can pitch in or step up.	The leader is on call 24/7; he or she has no backups or alternates, and no downtime to recharge, regroup, or re-energize.
Teams can efficiently develop replicable processes and create systems that can last over time; leadership practices are sustainable regardless of who is on the team.	A replicable process to sustain leadership capacity-building may be difficult to create with a lone leader; if the lone leader leaves, there is no one to pick up the torch.
This type of leadership builds capacity and re-energizes teams.	This type of leadership can drain energy, does not build capacity, and can deplete the leader's stamina.

There are many types of leaders and many styles of leadership. Some leadership styles achieve better results from followers than other styles do. Some followers respond better to one style over another. Effective school leaders know when and how to use the most appropriate leadership style depending on the situation and the people involved. Adapting or applying the required style of leadership to match a specific set of circumstances is referred to as *situational leadership* (DuFour et al., 2016).

Leaders of PLCs may go even further than simply adjusting their leadership styles in different situations. Effective PLC leaders know when and how to use the best leadership style in a situation as well as who on their guiding coalition would be the best person to take the lead. In a PLC, situations may require different personnel to lead at different times depending on what leadership strengths are required. When PLC principals call on others to use their leadership talents as situations call for them, that is known as *collaborative leadership* (Martin & Rains, 2018).

Collaborative leadership requires principals to share aspects of their leadership responsibilities with other personnel on staff. By sharing leadership and leveraging the talents of members of the team, PLC leaders can move commitment, accountability, and ownership deeper into their organizations.

Voices From the Field

I wish I had known the importance of training the guiding coalition members on how to be leaders. Most teachers don't know how to lead their colleagues. Good teacher leaders quickly realize how hard it is to work with adults sometimes. I think the biggest mistake we make is we throw teachers into leadership positions, and then we're disappointed when they are not leading the way we expect them to—when they may not know how to. Teachers didn't go to school to be leaders, so they need support, help, and confidence in how to lead their peers.

—Middle School Principal, Georgia

Douglas Reeves (2006), the founder of Creative Leadership Solutions, describes collaborative leadership as an oxymoron. Collaboration suggests sharing decision making with others and being inclusive, while leadership alludes to being solely in charge and making all the decisions. There are times when a leader requires immediate decisiveness. When a ship is sinking, that is not the time to assemble the crew and passengers on the bridge to vote on how to handle the situation. Outside of rare emergencies, Reeves (2006) recommends that leaders consider "some essential truths that mandate a collaborative approach" to leading PLCs:

- Employees in any organization are volunteers. We can compel their attendance and compliance, but only they can volunteer their hearts and minds.

- Leaders can make decisions with their authority, but they can implement those decisions only through collaboration.

- Leverage for improved organizational performance happens through networks, not individuals. If the only source of inspiration for improvement is the imprecations of the individual leader, then islands of excellence may result and be recognized, but long-term systemwide improvement will continue to be an illusion. (p. 52)

Collaborative leadership moves the members of your guiding coalition out of their grade-level or department-level silos so they can work together. Through the commitment to collaborative teamwork, the guiding coalition takes responsibility for leading the PLC process. This leadership model is in contrast to a more traditional top-down organizational structure, where a small group of administrators controls the process. When guiding coalitions represent all teams on campus, teams are energized, creativity is released, and the work culture becomes more productive and gratifying (Samur, 2019).

Transition Strategies

Transformation from lone to collaborative leadership takes time and requires patience. Moving from such traditional approaches and practices to collaborative teamwork does not happen at the flip of a switch. As your guiding coalition begins its work, it might want to consider the following transition strategies (Samur, 2019).

Clarify Your Primary Purpose for the Change

What is the guiding coalition's goal or primary purpose for transitioning to a more collaborative culture? In chapter 4, we explored part of the formula for creating a powerful guiding coalition: trust. Another part of the formula for transforming your leadership team into a powerful guiding coalition is for your team to identify its common purpose for becoming a PLC. Your goal or shared objective may be as simple as committing to excellence or creating a high-performing learning culture. Writing your guiding coalition's goal as a SMART goal will keep it in a short, uncomplicated, easy-to-follow format. Having no purpose can be a significant barrier to successful implementation.

When you create a team composed of the right people who trust each other and who work toward a shared objective, you create a *powerful* guiding coalition that is capable "to restructure, reengineer, or retool a set of strategies" (Kotter, 1996, p. 52).

Keep Communication Lines Open

Rather than depending on traditional school communication channels that travel along a chain of command (for example, through memos, emails, faculty meetings, team representatives, and so on), collaborative leadership depends on open lines of communication where all guiding coalition members express ideas and opinions and contribute to the discussion. Open communication is essential to collaboration. Collaborative leaders model behaviors that show appreciation for others and engage them in purposeful conversations.

Build Partnership Skills

Most PLC initiatives begin with the best of intentions; if they do falter or fail, it may be due to a lack of partnership skills. Partnership skills within the guiding coalition refer to the acknowledgment that each team member will bring different experiences to the team. This diversity of experiences strengthens and enriches the collaborative leadership team. As different as they are, all experiences are accepted and valid. To be in partnership with the members of your guiding coalition, you cannot use your positional power to minimize a team member's experience or to make it undiscussable. Doing so negates the power of the partnering aspect required of a collaborative team.

Don't Waste Time

Transformation is a messy and complex process. You spend a great deal of time learning the PLC process, building trust, and building shared knowledge. Even if your team is making seismic changes to your school's structure and processes, you don't necessarily completely dismantle everything that is currently in place. Your team can save time, effort, and resources if you identify what the school currently has in place that contributes to collaborative practices. You need not change these aspects. Your task will be to add collaborative leadership practices to whatever positives are already embedded in the school's culture. For example, your teams may already have dedicated time in their weekly schedule to meet collaboratively, so you would not need to adjust your schedule. However, your teams may not be using their collaborative team time wisely (focusing on the four critical questions, developing CFAs, and so on). Another example is that your teams created norms but do not use them or refer to them. Perhaps they did not develop accountability protocols to address violations of the norms.

Don't Be Afraid to Show Vulnerability

When leading your guiding coalition, you may find this last strategy the most difficult to practice. Collaborative leadership is all about *we*. It can never be about *me*. When refocusing from me to we, school leaders need to let down their guard. Collaborating at the leadership level is a clear signal to your guiding coalition members that you don't have all the answers, and you need their assistance and expertise in finding them. Collaborative leadership creates a high-risk, high-reward situation for principals and team members because approachability and vulnerability are at stake. PLC leaders tend to be more approachable and vulnerable than traditional school leaders. Collaborative leaders check their egos at the door to engage others in problem solving and consensus building that ensure better solutions.

Use the PLC Block-and-Tackle System

When lifting heavy objects, you can move a limited amount of weight by yourself. An effective way to move heavy objects is by using pulleys—simple machines that make it easier to move and lift objects. When you utilize a system called a *block and tackle* to multiply the lifting potential of a set of pulleys, the pulleys can handle incredible amounts of weight. For example, a block and tackle makes it possible for a sailor to manage the force of wind and move the sails to steer his boat.

Your guiding coalition is much like a complex block-and-tackle system. Powerful guiding coalitions have the potential to move enormously heavy loads when they securely anchor the loads to the school's mission, vision, values (collective commitments), and goals. We know a single principal or even a small handful of school administrators cannot lead a collaborative culture as effectively as a guiding coalition can. The best way to lead a PLC is by applying a block-and-tackle system of team leaders. By encouraging your guiding coalition to engage in pull leadership, you will be better able to lift the leadership weight of your PLC. Like the ropes of a complex block-and-tackle system, the members of your guiding coalition will help lift the weight so that you and your administrative team will not break your backs.

When moving your school's culture from one that values isolation to one that embraces collaboration and teamwork, all members of your collaborative learning teams, in addition to those on the guiding coalition, are to be (Mattos et al., 2016):

- Assigned to meaningful teams rather than artificial teams (Since time to meet in meaningful teams is precious, principals may wish to limit the number of formal teams that staff members can join. For example, members of the guiding coalition might serve on their grade-level or department-level team in addition to the guiding coalition. Keeping the number of formal teams to a manageable number can help keep personnel from burning out. Limiting the number of formal teams your staff serve on can also provide them with a bit more wiggle room to allow them to serve on less formal and less time-consuming ad hoc committees.)

- Provided with adequate time to collaborate regularly (Specific times are reserved for the guiding coalition to meet. Many high-performing guiding coalitions meet weekly, especially at the beginning of their PLC journey.)

- Crystal clear on the work required of them (It is for this reason the guiding coalition has a common goal to guide its leadership responsibilities. This common goal will bind the guiding coalition together to create a powerful leadership team.)

- Provided with oversight, resources, and support to ensure their success

By ensuring the guiding coalition is properly structured and established from its inception, team members will gain experiences and practice meeting expectations that they can model in their collaborative team meetings.

At the beginning of the PLC journey, the guiding coalition ensures the following during its development and during the establishment of the teams it represents (Mattos et al., 2016).

- **Personnel are required to meet collaboratively, not just encouraged to do so:** To succeed, the school must embed collaboration in its regular practice. Working collaboratively must be required of all personnel, including guiding coalition members and administrators.

- **Personnel must operate as teams, not groups:** To model proper teamwork, the guiding coalition must ensure it has all required elements of a team in place and it regularly practices them in its work and then passes them on to the teams it represents. The guiding coalition establishes and works toward its common goal. It practices and models working interdependently. Members practice and model being mutually accountable to each other. Practicing and experiencing these three elements will help create a strong guiding coalition and provide guiding coalition members with a model to follow when leading their teams.

- **Teams must focus on the right work:** When the guiding coalition focuses on the right work (the three big ideas of a PLC and the four critical questions), its members become better equipped to successfully carry that focus into their collaborative team meetings.

Review, Redo, and Renew (Re³)

Positive impact and change expert Susan C. Young (n.d.) shares a process called *review, redo, and renew*, or *Re³*. It involves reviewing previous experience, redoing or revising what was not effective or worthwhile, and feeling renewed as a result of success the second time around. Leaders and leadership teams can benefit from this Re3 philosophy.

An example of how your guiding coalition might use Re3 might be after a problem-solving session where your team is working through how collaborative teams might develop and use an effective agenda template during their collaborative team time. After using a proposed agenda template format for the first few meetings, the guiding coalition decides to discuss what is working and what is getting in the way of holding successful meetings. Several teams felt the team norms needed to be included in the agenda template because they were not reviewing them at the beginning of the meeting nor were they posted anywhere. Their teams were not including norms in their meeting process. After the guiding coalition reviewed what these teams were experiencing, it was decided that the agenda planning template would be revised to include the norms on the form for reference. Once the change was agreed to, the guiding coalition celebrated the fact that they were able to solve the problem for fellow team members. The team felt renewed and excited that their collaboration led to a useful solution.

Mindset

Leaders can effectively move school cultures from traditional to collaborative leadership by developing, recognizing, and encouraging growth mindsets in themselves, their staff, and their students. People with a growth mindset see challenges and changes as motivators that increase effort and learning. Focusing on growth mindsets and the language of growth mindsets can contribute to facilitating positive attitudes and beliefs that staff members have the capacity, power, and control to make positive cultural changes (Dweck, 2016). PLC leaders should nourish growth mindsets about student learning and teacher collaboration so those mindsets can thrive and flourish.

Unlike growth mindsets, fixed mindsets and fixed mindset language are held and used by people who believe their traits, skills, and characteristics are limited. For example, they believe intelligence, talent, and confidence are fixed traits. They think they are born with static personal traits that can never change or improve. They believe talent alone creates success. Unfortunately, they believe they cannot succeed in certain areas. Fixed mindsets create a feeling of helplessness and inadequacy. Individuals with fixed mindsets feel paralyzed and unable to make positive changes in areas that they consider to be weaknesses.

A third type of mindset, which is based on psychologist Carol Dweck's (2016) work and was developed by George Couros, is an innovator's mindset (Froehlich, 2019). Those who empower others to marvel and to examine the world around them hold an innovator's mindset. In addition to freeing you from a fixed mindset that freezes your focus and emphasis on what can limit you, this mindset can help you become a leader who is forward thinking.

Table 5.2 compares how individuals with different mindsets approach or view situations that commonly challenge them. The mindset through which they view each situation can determine their behaviors and actions.

Table 5.2: How Individuals With Different Mindsets View Different Situations

Situation	Fixed Mindset	Growth Mindset	Innovator's Mindset
Challenges	They avoid challenges to maintain the appearance of intelligence.	They embrace challenges stemming from a desire to learn.	They seek out challenges that they see as opportunities for growth and development.
Obstacles	Giving up in the face of obstacles and setbacks is a common response.	Showing perseverance in the face of obstacles and setbacks is a common response.	When obstacles arise, they shift their thinking to look for opportunities and possibilities.
Effort	They view having to try or put in effort as a negative; they believe if you have to try, you're not very smart or talented.	They believe working hard and putting in effort pave the path to achievement and success.	They believe hard work and effort are continuous, and it's important to make time to create new solutions and ideas for growth.
Criticism	They view criticism as negative feedback regardless of how constructive it is, and they ignore it.	They view criticism as providing important feedback that can aid in learning.	They view criticism as providing important feedback that creates the opportunity to implement new and better ideas for learning from others.
Success of others	They see other people's success as a threat that evokes feelings of insecurity or vulnerability.	They see other people's success as a source of inspiration and education.	They see other people's success as something to learn from and modify and apply to their own context to create success.

Source: Adapted from Froehlich, 2019.

Leading with a growth mindset means encouraging your staff and facilitating the belief that they have the capacity and talent to change. Effectively delivering this positive message stands squarely on your shoulders; only you have the authority and responsibility to make the initial cultural course correcting required at the onset of the

PLC journey. However, it is *never* your responsibility to do all the cultural tweaking, reculturing, and reworking alone. It is your guiding coalition's responsibility to assist and support you.

Voices From the Field

The two things that all members [of the guiding coalition] had to have were an open mind and a growth mindset. I encouraged and wanted people who would question and challenge ideas. The one thing you have to be careful of is what the entire group's dynamics are when they are all together. I definitely had some "late adopters" on the team, but they were learners. If they were not open to change or challenging the status quo, I would not place them on the team, with one exception. The exception is having your union leadership as a part of the team. It was extremely beneficial to put my union leadership around a team of teachers who were learning, studying successful schools, and wanting to improve outcomes.

—Assistant Superintendent for Curriculum and Instruction, California

Leadership for All Faculty Personalities

Just as leaders have different styles of leading, staff members have different strengths and liabilities. To help facilitate your school staff through PLC transformation and to strengthen the school's foundation and culture building, you will need to lead all types of faculty personalities. Knowing people's strengths and liabilities and how to weave those characteristics to create a strong cultural fabric can bolster your leadership effectiveness. The initial leadership challenge is to determine how to get faculty members with varied personality styles and degrees of knowledge, motivation, and experience to move together in a new direction.

Don Lowry (n.d.) developed a system for identifying and understanding people's personality temperaments, which he calls True Colors; the True Colors system uses four colors to represent and differentiate four distinct personality styles. According to Lowry (n.d.), every person is a unique blend of the four colors or styles—orange, blue, gold, and green—that he describes as a spectrum. No colors in the system are bad or good, right or wrong; they simply provide insight into people's motivations, actions, and approaches to communication.

In *Leadership Styles: A Behavioral Matrix*, researcher Susan Sayers (1978) refers to four styles similar to Lowry's, using descriptive terms instead of colors. Her behavioral matrix describes the styles as promoter (Lowry's orange), supporter (Lowry's blue), controller (Lowry's gold), and analyzer (Lowry's green; Sayers, 1978). Think of these colors and names of styles as descriptive words to distinguish the four basic types. Leaders who understand the interaction and power of the four styles can better lead and communicate the PLC concepts to all staff members.

The Oranges (Promoters)

Some team members are ready and willing to adopt and welcome change. They are motivated, action oriented, and impulsive. They are likely to embrace change even before the purpose or details are shared. These individuals generally make quick decisions and take advantage of immediate opportunities. They learn best when offered activity and movement. They tend to be the ones who assemble toys and furniture without reading the instructions. They usually raise their hands to volunteer at faculty meetings without knowing what they are volunteering for. Their motto might be, "Fire, ready, aim!"

The Blues (Supporters)

The second type of team member is emotionally driven and seeks harmony among team members. These team members seek contentment and physical tranquility. Once they are assured everyone is comfortable and safe, they are ready to contribute to the team effort. They are there when you need them and will go the extra mile for others. At faculty meetings, they are the ones who make sure goodies are on the media center tables and everyone feels welcome. Their slogan might be, "Ready, ready, ready, aim, fire!"

The Golds (Controllers)

The third type of team member is highly organized. These team members value stability, responsibility, efficiency, and thoroughness. They may keep bulleted lists, maintain detailed schedules, and arrive at meetings on the dot—no sooner, no later. Perhaps with a little help from a carpenter's level, they may check to make sure the bottoms of their bath towels hang perfectly straight. They might organize their pantries alphabetically and by size, weight, and food group. They might jokingly suggest that there are two ways of doing things: their way or the wrong way. Their rallying cry might be, "Ready, aim, fire, fire, fire!"

The Greens (Analyzers)

The fourth type of team member may require more time before getting on board, not because these team members are against anything but because they need to gather and digest as much information as possible before making a decision. They generally have a calming and composed demeanor and use mind over emotion to manage and solve life's mysteries. Their strength lies in thinking logically and analyzing data before accepting change. They value knowledge and information. Their bookshelves are chock-full of books, so much so that they have a second row of books and manuals hiding behind the visible row of books and manuals. At faculty meetings, when others have completed a given task and start talking, these individuals are still reading the instructions. Perhaps their motto could be, "Aim, aim, aim, ready, fire!"

Each color has its strengths and drawbacks depending on the situation, the interaction, and other factors. Teams made with members of all four colors can be unstoppable.

Knowing the characteristics of the colors or styles provides insight into different approaches to motivation, action, and communication among team members. These differences do not have to drive team members apart. Understanding and celebrating the differences among staff members ultimately strengthen teams when led effectively. Using True Colors or similar style assessments may prove useful to leaders who wish to better learn how to successfully lead different styles with different needs in the same direction. Visit the True Colors International website (https://truecolorsintl.com /the-four-color-personalities) to learn more about the True Colors style assessments. Leaders and team members can use such assessment information to determine their styles, including their individual leadership strengths and limitations; follower behaviors; and pros and cons of interactions among the styles.

To ensure ownership by a diverse staff, assessing and understanding individual needs, strengths, and potential liabilities are critical at the beginning of the PLC journey. The good news is that PLCs benefit from the talents that staff of all the styles bring to the table. All people bring individual expertise and perspectives, and all styles have their strengths and liabilities.

Voices From the Field

I didn't have a clue about what I was getting into in terms of creating a guiding coalition. I gathered a group of people who were passionate about the same thing I was—student learning. We formed a team and decided how we were going to move the school forward into this new era. I guess some of the things I would've liked to have known better are things like ensuring that personalities match and that we have a healthy combination of different types of people on the team. Also, I think it's important to spend time in team-building exercises so that we really get to know and trust each other. There are a number of websites that offer instructions for team-building and trust-building activities specifically for school personnel.

—High School Principal, California

Movement at the Right Pace

Since school staff have a mixture of educators with many diverse gifts, talents, and liabilities, the leader's challenge becomes how to move the whole staff toward change in an organized, positive way and at a not too fast or too slow pace. How do school leaders move at the perfect pace so they don't lose those who believe change is moving too quickly and those who think transformation is not moving quickly enough?

How do school leaders get ownership from a staff of eager oranges who are champing at the bit, ready and rarin' to move forward; sensitive blues who want to ensure the environment is just right before moving to something new; highly structured golds who want to move in an organized, disciplined way, by the numbers and by the book; and cautious greens who need to have things slowed down so that they can process the information and research on PLCs? If leaders tend to lead in their color, how will they be able to bring the other colors on board?

For example, how will a gold leader build shared knowledge with the blues? Solely giving a structured, bulleted presentation may not be the best means to sell the basic concepts of and research on PLCs. However, appealing to the affective benefits of PLCs might make the change more attractive.

If a green leader communicates the advantages of becoming a PLC by providing only information and data, the message might not reach the oranges, or it might turn them off. Perhaps sharing the exciting changes that PLCs enjoy after implementation will motivate oranges to hop on board. Allowing oranges to visit a neighboring PLC that is enjoying successful implementation and reporting their observations to staff might be a better option.

Table 5.3 shows strategies that are useful for leading and collaborating with the different styles.

Table 5.3: Sample Strategies for Leading and Collaborating With Different Styles

Promoters (Oranges)	Supporters (Blues)	Controllers (Golds)	Analyzers (Greens)
• Work in teams, pairs, or triads; work in committees. • Encourage movement. • Use turn-and-talk to process information. • Use brainstorming. • Use role-playing activities. • Include humor.	• Greet and introduce team members. • Use icebreakers. • Take breaks. • Provide snacks. • Celebrate. • Recognize individuals and teams for their efforts. • Use group-learning activities that encourage participation by all staff members. • Allow for staff to share personal stories and testimonials.	• Use agendas. • Announce decision-making options. • Announce team roles. • Start on time and end on time. • Announce and get agreement on ground rules. • Use graphic organizers. • Give opportunities to facilitate.	• Provide data. • Give time to process information. • Provide reviews and wrap-ups. • Give time for reflection, clarification, and questions and answers. • Give desired outcomes and learning outcomes. • Provide research-based information, bibliographies, and references.

A staff with many different personalities, strengths, and limitations is a staff that has incredible potential. The more diverse the staff is, the stronger and more resilient it can become.

Conclusion

As your leadership moves from leadership by one (or by a small administrator-only team) to a collaborative team, you do not give up or let go of responsibility or authority. Rather, you gain and increase your scope of responsibility and authority as you share the leadership efforts. Collaborative leadership allows you to leverage your leadership responsibilities through the members of your guiding coalition. When effective guiding coalitions stay true to their commitments and the PLC basics, collaborative leadership seeps into the teacher teams. Adding more, but not too many, people to your decision-making team, your guiding coalition, means you have more chefs in the kitchen or officers on the bridge. Collaborative leadership takes time and effort compared to leadership by one because it increases the number of people involved and the amount of time to share information and make decisions. Although processes initially seem to slow up because of the additional time it takes to involve more people, they will speed up once your guiding coalition learns to work together more effectively and efficiently. The motto, "go slow to go fast," describes the process to move from a single leader to a collaborative leadership team. If collaborative leadership were a kitchen appliance, it would be a slow cooker. The work simmers and stews.

Chapter 6 highlights four PLC leadership levers that, when applied, can help you grow and sustain the leadership capacity of your guiding coalition and staff. When your PLC focuses on leadership development and sustainability, the collaborative culture you established will have an excellent chance of enduring beyond your leadership tenure.

▶ Next Steps

Using table 5.1 (page 108), assess whether you are depending more on the leadership of your guiding coalition or that of yourself as the lone leader. If the lone leader column describes much of your leadership, determine what you could do to develop a more collaborative leadership style. Create an action plan using the three-step goal-setting process found on page 51. How will you know if your efforts make a difference?

? FAQs

Collaborative leadership, leading through a guiding coalition versus managing a team, sounds awesome; however, many times when I pass tasks to my leadership team, I find that I make more work for myself because I am constantly following up and checking on everyone's progress. Where do I begin to let them lead their teams?

Start slowly. For example, one of their first responsibilities might be to create team norms. After you have led your guiding coalition through the process to develop and approve its norms, let your team members know that it is now their turn to each take their grade level or department through the same process. Review with your guiding coalition members the process you used with them and its purpose. Discuss and determine a deadline for all teams to turn in drafts for review. Allow them to ask questions so they become comfortable with the process.

Once you have given your team members their task, turn them loose, and make yourself available for support, resources, and assistance. Informally check in with them, and assist where necessary. After all drafts are submitted, bring the guiding coalition back for the Re3 process to review, redo, and renew. What went well? What got in the way? What leadership best practices can your team share? Let the team members learn from each other.

Yes, having them lead the norm creation process (or any team process for that matter) without your being in the room to watch every move certainly comes with risks; but even mama birds run a huge risk when they coax their babies out of their nests for their first flight.

I agree that attitudes and mindsets have a huge impact on how well my guiding coalition works together. I have a few team members who have a fixed mindset about PLCs because our school previously attempted to implement the process a few years ago, before I came. From what I understand, it was dreadful because the principal controlled the process rather than led the process through a collaborative leadership team. How might I consider reintroducing the PLC concept to my staff without turning them off at the very beginning?

You might want to approach the situation from this perspective: "Based on what we know about the impact of PLCs on student learning, we are going to learn and lead as a unified guiding coalition. What's been done in the past is behind us. We are making a fresh start, and the beauty of how we are approaching the process is that everyone on the leadership team is on the front line to ensure everything the school does this time is done well."

Make sure you build shared knowledge with your guiding coalition members about the research and the school's current reality; and most important, give them the why behind the work required to transform the school into a PLC. Your positive attitude, your growth mindset, and your enthusiasm about the potential for change can be infectious. When you see or hear members still engaged in fixed-mindset behaviors or comments, meet individually with them to reassure them that with their help and support, this change will make the difference. Look for the little opportunities where you can reinforce members' work and their positive work attitude.

I like having information about personality styles. It helps me ensure that I am meeting everyone's needs and not leaving out a specific style. My concern is that I do not have anyone on my guiding coalition who is an orange. When my guiding coalition uses the styles planning template, how do we honor the orange perspective without having someone with that perspective on the team?

You should ensure that your team represents missing styles. If no one on the guiding coalition is an orange, the team must ensure that it still considers the orange perspective or point of view because all team members are a combination of all four colors. All four colors must be in the room whether in person or in spirit. The guiding coalition should create a list of possible questions an orange would ask and a list of possible actions an orange would take if he or she were in the room. Your team might wish to use the styles-planning tool (see the example in figure 5.1, page 122) to include the orange perspective during any team-related process or activity. As the guiding coalition goes through the process to brainstorm strategies for working with oranges in figure 5.1, the team will be viewing the activity and session goals through the perspective of the promoters or oranges. This "participants' perspective" keeps team members from wanting to focus on activities and strategies that might meet their individual styles' needs. Completing figure 5.1 gives them the opportunity to view the activities while standing in the oranges' shoes. Ensuring the four voices are in the room will guarantee that you consider all faculty and staff members' perspectives.

A couple of teachers on our guiding coalition are struggling when leading their collaborative teams. One teacher reported her team was not taking ownership of the PLC concepts and process. The other teacher said her team was constantly getting off track and ending up in the weeds. How do I advise these teachers?

There are several ways to approach these situations. One possible solution is to have them bring their issues before the guiding coalition for discussion and assistance. In the collaborative leadership setting, the team can brainstorm ideas for the two leaders. (Refer to figure 2.3, page 47.) The other team members can share similar experiences they have had along with their solutions to the same issues. Another approach you could take, if these teachers' issues are serious, is you or one of your team leaders may attend the team meetings to see what support the teams might need. Finally, if there does not appear to be any internal resource to address this concern, perhaps a principal colleague in your district who has encountered similar challenges may be able to attend one of your guiding coalition meetings and share with your team how he or she addressed the challenges.

The overriding style of my guiding coalition is gold. The members are drivers. They tend to push the PLC concepts even when their teams are not ready to move on. As a result, tension, frustration, and even hurt feelings are cropping up in several teams. How do I handle this?

If your guiding coalition has not had professional learning in how to lead different styles, you may wish to start there. Understanding the strengths and the liabilities of

What is the activity, presentation, project, assignment, or task?	A half-day overview by the guiding coalition of the four critical questions for all collaborative learning teams
How will you ensure that the needs of the promoters (oranges) will be met?	Work in teams, pairs, or triads. Use brainstorming. Role-play. Encourage movement. Engage in activities. Include humor.
How will you ensure that the needs of the supporters (blues) will be met?	Start with introductions. Provide snacks. Take breaks. Use icebreakers. Greet participants. Have celebrations or recognitions.
How will you ensure that the needs of the controllers (golds) will be met?	Use agendas. Announce team roles. Start on time and end on time. Announce decision-making options. Announce and get agreement on ground rules. Use graphic organizers.
How will you ensure that the needs of the analyzers (greens) will be met?	Provide data. Give time to process information. Give desired outcomes and learning outcomes. Provide reviews and wrap-ups. Give time for reflection, clarification, and questions and answers. Provide research-based information, bibliographies, and references.

FIGURE 5.1: Sample styles-planning template.

*Visit **go.SolutionTree.com/PLCbooks** for a free reproducible version of this figure.*

their own style may prove very beneficial to the guiding coalition members. When they understand how their style affects the other styles on their team, they will better understand how their leadership is perceived. For example, a gold leader may introduce a specific concept or task that the team must accomplish. When a green follower sees and hears the information, he or she may need more time to process what the leader is asking of the team. Gold leaders are at risk of running right over greens to check the task off the list and move on; understanding the green perspective will help them prevent this.

Understanding the styles and building in ways they all can work together in a team setting are critical to the success of your teams and your PLC journey. Once your guiding coalition understands how different styles best work together, it may recommend styles training for the entire staff.

Reflection

Reflect on an upcoming activity, presentation, project, assignment, or task. Using figure 5.1 as a reference, complete the "Styles-Planning Template" (page 124). This tool will help you and your guiding coalition plan how to meet the learning needs of each of the four styles.

Styles-Planning Template

What is the activity, presentation, project, assignment, or task?	
How will you ensure that the needs of the promoters (oranges) will be met?	
How will you ensure that the needs of the supporters (blues) will be met?	
How will you ensure that the needs of the controllers (golds) will be met?	
How will you ensure that the needs of the analyzers (greens) will be met?	

CHAPTER 6
LEVERAGING YOUR LEADERSHIP

As we learn and grow together, the collective strength of our professional learning community is enhanced, and our students are the beneficiaries.

—Linda Bowgren and Kathryn Sever

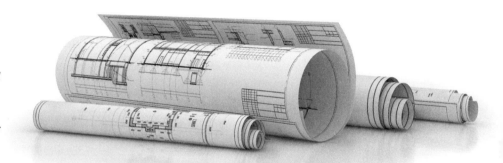

Most people will acknowledge that it takes great will and strength of character to break habits—especially bad ones—and transition into new habits. Leaders of PLCs are transition leaders (Stewart, 2016)—they seek to sever the flow of negative or harmful traditions and practices that have passed from generation to generation in their schools.

A transition leader acts in much the same way as a person born into a family with a history of unhealthy relationships or behaviors who seeks to replace those negative and unhealthy behaviors with positive ways of being. He or she might intentionally behave in healthy ways and snuff out the long line of destructive behaviors that have plagued the family.

Likewise, as your school's transition leader, you commit to stopping the flow of behaviors, attitudes, and actions that have kept students from achieving at high levels in your school. Once you know what best practices, strategies, and processes can elevate student learning and teacher effectiveness, you commit to doing better and to leading those around you to do the same. The guiding coalition has the potential to become a high-performing team of transition leaders who, like you, are ready, willing, and able to break the cycle of bad practices and ineffectiveness that has been allowed to exist for too long.

This chapter explores some leadership levers to help you and your guiding coalition transition from a traditional school structure to a PLC structure. Leadership levers help reduce the amount of leadership effort required of school leaders. These PLC leadership levers can multiply, enhance, or strengthen your leadership. Applying these levers can create a powerful, synergistic school culture. It begins with the lever of leading the learning.

Lead the Learning

Effective professional learning begins with you, the principal, as the lead learner. Your commitment, enthusiasm, and passion for learning and improvement will extend to your guiding coalition. When guiding coalition members also focus on creating learning opportunities for their collaborative teacher teams, it increases the likelihood that the staff as a whole will embrace and respond to the learning required to move your school forward. As Richard DuFour and Robert Marzano (2011) note, "Great leaders are great learners" (p. 198).

Leading the professional learning means bridging the knowing-doing gap (Pfeffer & Sutton, 2000), moving from research to action. Leaders can do this by providing professional learning at the personal, guiding coalition, and collaborative team levels (Learning Forward, n.d.a).

At the Personal Level

A professional learning community implies a community of learners. In such a community, "the principal is the leader of learning, the one who leads the school community in learning about and implementing best practices and ensuring a culture of continuous learning and improvement" (DuFour et al., 2016, p. 247). Principals and their guiding coalitions are expected to actively participate in ongoing professional learning. They are also expected to provide frequent professional learning for their collaborative teams.

Effective PLC leaders:

- View professional learning as an important approach for supporting essential school and school system improvements

- Identify learning among their top priorities for students, staff, and themselves

- Make their own personal and professional learning visible to other stakeholders

- Participate in professional learning provided by internal and external sources

- Model expected attitudes and behaviors for others (Learning Forward, n.d.a)

At the Guiding Coalition Level

Leadership provides the necessary framework to create and sustain PLCs. Leaders of PLCs "must believe that people can learn and grow together, and must be willing to invest whatever allows that bonding to take place" (Blankstein et al., 2008, p. 161).

Effective PLC leaders:

- Foster colleague-to-colleague support for professional learning and ensure a steady focus on shared goals (Learning Forward, n.d.b)

- Facilitate professional learning or coach and advise those who lead it (Learning Forward, n.d.a)

- Create a norms-based culture based on high expectations, shared responsibility, mutual respect, and high levels of trust (Learning Forward, n.d.a)

- Encourage all personnel to engage in effective job-embedded or external professional learning to meet established goals (Learning Forward, n.d.a)

At the Collaborative Team Level

As Shirley Hord and William Sommers (2008) explain in their book *Leading Professional Learning Communities: Voices From Research and Practice*:

> Leaders make a difference. They make a difference through their leadership capacity to affect the system around them and on the future of the organization. We want to state that leadership teams and teacher leaders, both formal and informal, are critical in moving the school into professional learning communities. (pp. 27–28)

Effective PLC leaders:

- Ensure school teams meet frequently to engage in collaborative professional learning that enhances their practice and increases student results (Learning Forward, n.d.b)

- Ensure team members are mutually accountable to each other to achieve shared goals (Learning Forward, n.d.b)

- Ensure team members are collectively responsible for the learning of all students within the school (Learning Forward, n.d.b)

- Encourage team members to share best practices by visiting each other's classrooms and sharing resources (Learning Forward, n.d.b)

- Require teams to develop norms and to use processes and structures that help teams analyze, plan, implement, support, and evaluate their professional practice (Learning Forward, n.d.b)

As educational researcher Michael Fullan (2003) notes, all organizations need to be learning organizations to be effective. In a school, the principal has to be the lead learner. "If principals do not go out of their way to learn more (inside and outside of the school), regardless of what the system is doing they cannot become a pressure point for positive change" (Fullan, 2003, p. 20).

The purpose behind the concept of principals being the lead learner is not so they become the sole beneficiaries of the learning. Principals who do not share the learning or encourage professional learning in those they lead deny the guiding coalition and their collaborative teams the potential benefits derived from the learning. Being a lead learner is about sharing the learning with others so that the school becomes a learning organization. Sharing learning results in an environment of continuous improvement gives focus to the purpose of a PLC: learning for all.

In a PLC, principals see themselves as the lead learner. They are the person to whom students and staff look as the model for learning. Learning-focused principals ensure that learning and leading occur at the same time in the same place. They are not competing entities.

When creating a learning culture, PLC principals and their guiding coalitions put the topic of professional learning on their agendas to answer the question, "What are we going to do to ensure professional learning becomes a top priority in our school?" The answers to this question will help school leaders make time for professional learning and not allow it to become an afterthought or an add-on. Responding to the question about professional learning also gives the guiding coalition the opportunity to see if there are any time-wasting activities in the schedule that can be eliminated. Making time for professional learning does not require filling that time with additional meetings or in-service trainings. Making more time for collaborative teams to meet can increase opportunities for ongoing, job-embedded learning and sharing of best practices.

> If the bad news is that principals have less time than ever to devote to their own learning, the good news is that they are making time. They no longer need to apologize for including themselves in the learning communities over which they preside. In fact, rather than tiptoeing out the back of the room once they begin a staff development program for others, school principals now commonly participate and model the most important activity of the schoolhouse—learning. (Barth, 2001, p. 148)

Voices From the Field

> What role does our guiding coalition play? Our guiding coalition still plays a role in helping to create and facilitate our professional development. It also helps to facilitate our mission and vision and helps to create goals based on our continuous improvement plan.
>
> —Middle School Principal, Ohio

Develop Courageous Followers

Leaders and followers depend on each other for any organization or team to succeed. Without Batman, would we have ever heard of Robin? As explored in chapter 4 (page 87), the leader-follower relationship tends to be more of a boss-employee interaction in traditional school structures. In PLCs, the line between leaders and followers is less distinct because the very nature of collaborative cultures requires working together and supporting each other for the benefit of the whole.

Ira Chaleff, author of *The Courageous Follower* (Chaleff, 2009), suggests that "the days of all-powerful leaders and subservient followers are long gone" (Welcome, 2019). Leaders and followers cannot attain their highest levels of effectiveness without each other. Their relationship seems to take on the qualities found in *mutualism*, a type of symbiosis where both parties are mutually dependent on each other and benefit from the relationship.

It requires great courage for you to lead your school through PLC transformation; such weighty change, however, cannot depend on your talents alone. To strengthen the cumulative leadership effort, those who follow you, especially those on your guiding coalition, also need courage. (The importance of the courageous follower role is introduced in the "Avoiding Elephant Traps" section of chapter 1, page 23.)

As Chaleff (Welcome, 2019) observes in his Courageous Follower model, followers do not serve leaders; rather, followers and leaders serve a common purpose, a mission, and they do it within the boundaries created by a set of shared values. When school personnel lead and follow courageously, the initiatives and processes they pursue are enhanced exponentially. As principal, you might wish to review the dimensions of courageous followership (figure 6.1) to see if there is a member of your guiding coalition whom you might approach to serve in this capacity.

Dimensions of Courageous Followership

Assume responsibility: Exercise self-accountability to "create opportunities to fulfill your potential and maximize your value to the organization."

Serve: Work hard to support the leader while remaining as passionate as the leader in pursuing the organization's mission.

Challenge: Be willing to respectfully voice your concerns in uncomfortable situations, such as when contradicting leaders.

Participate: Create transformations by being adaptable and embracing change.

Take moral action: Challenge a leader's position by doing something different because it is the right thing to do.

Speak to the hierarchy: Be comfortable openly communicating with leaders at all levels of the organization.

Source: Welcome, 2019.

FIGURE 6.1: Chaleff's dimensions of courageous followership.

Courageous followers are mission driven rather than personality driven. Some members of your guiding coalition may not be willing or able to fulfill the role of the courageous follower. That's to be expected. However, if you can lead one or two team members in assuming this vital role, your guiding coalition will undoubtedly benefit; and the effectiveness of your leadership will strengthen as well.

Harness the Potential and Power of Teacher Leadership

While your car's engine is running, the alternator charges the battery and powers the electrical system. Without the alternator, the battery would eventually die (Goeres, 2017). Teacher leadership is the alternator for your PLC—it helps propel your PLC toward your school's vision. It also creates and stores the energy to build the leadership capacity that your school will require in the future. Without a purposeful emphasis on teacher leadership, your school will have no way of storing power for later use when it is needed. Depending solely on your guiding coalition to help lead your PLC could be harmful down the road. If you do not provide your classroom teachers with leadership opportunities, you could potentially stunt your school's ability to build capacity and ensure long-term sustainability.

The PLC process must have the built-in means to develop and sustain leadership within the teacher ranks. Otherwise, there is a real possibility that some staff members will work themselves into the ground while others' talents go untapped. PLCs do not depend on the leadership of a dedicated few; they require contributions, regardless of how large or small, from every staff member. When enlisting all teachers to help lead, you may wish to consider reframing the focus on leadership as a focus on professional contribution in case you are concerned the formal term *leadership* will frighten some of your faculty.

Authors Marilyn Katzenmeyer and Gayle Moller have compared tapping into the leadership potential of classroom teachers to waking a sleeping giant. PLC schools take advantage of this tremendous resource and use it to help lead the guiding coalition and the collaborative teacher teams. Many times, school leaders look everywhere for new sources of leadership only to learn that there is unlimited potential within their school that can make a significant impact on the speed and extent of school transformation (Katzenmeyer & Moller, 2009). Formally providing leadership opportunities for your staff can keep the leadership pipeline flowing as members of your guiding coalition retire, are promoted, or move off the team to give new members a chance to lead. Table 6.1 (page 132) offers some potential teacher leadership opportunities at three levels of risk: (1) low, (2) medium, and (3) high. When considering participating in these opportunities, teachers weigh several risks of taking advantage of them. Teachers may ask, "Is this opportunity too much to assume at this time? What if I fail at participating in this opportunity, task, or activity? Will this opportunity lead me in the right direction of my own professional growth? Will participating in this activity take me further out of my comfort zone than I am willing to go at this time?"

Exposure to leadership opportunities provides teachers with two distinct resources from which they can learn and benefit: (1) the results of work they do and (2) the experiences they gain from the work. Teachers can later draw from these stored experiences to enhance the overall leadership capacity of the school.

There is a saying attributed to Greek philosopher Heraclitus: "You cannot step in the same stream twice." In the context of developing leadership and leadership opportunities, the saying can describe the stream of numerous opportunities that pass by you and your teacher leaders every day—responsibilities, tasks, and challenges. People standing on the bank of the stream look at the flow of opportunities swiftly passing by. Each chooses whether they should step into the leadership stream to take on a specific task, responsibility, position, or experience. Their decision to step in or to stay on the bank could be determined by a number of factors: the level of certain risks they might assume; the amount of time the task or activity might take; whether or not they will require support, professional development, or training to prepare for the opportunity; or whether or not the experience is congruent with their professional development goals and aspirations.

Table 6.1 lists some of the incredible leadership opportunities flowing by your staff members every day. Are they prepared to step into the stream, or should they wait? Do they require more experience and preparation? As their principal, you might want to coach them and help them recognize these opportunities and determine which are the most appropriate for their leadership growth and development.

Sustaining the cultural changes brought about when creating a PLC necessitates both lateral and vertical capacity building (Fullan, 2006). This allows for the development of teacher leadership within the school and encourages the promotion of eligible school-based leaders to district-level positions as they become vacant. To encourage capacity building at the school level, principals can employ the same strategies they use to build PLCs: leading data-driven decision-making initiatives or action research allows teachers to work with data and focus on the process of building shared knowledge. Leading collaborative teams strengthens teacher leaders' skills in team organization, communication, and facilitation. Providing job-embedded professional learning to teams or a whole faculty gives teacher leaders excellent opportunities to share their expertise and best practices with staff. Allowing teacher leaders to assist or coach teams or team leaders who are struggling with leading their collaborative work can strengthen decision-making and problem-solving skills.

Throughout the year, principals may wish to consider providing substitute teachers to free up teacher leaders so they can take advantage of available leadership-development and school-improvement opportunities. Giving teacher leaders opportunities beyond the school day to volunteer leading or supervising after-school activities, sports events, and so on can be a great way for them to gain leadership experience. Collaborative teams may also offer ideas on how to group their classes for a short period of time to give teacher leaders an opportunity to break free to participate in a leadership activity or experience.

Create a Legacy of Leadership

Whether or not you realize it, as principal, you are connected to generations of school leaders who came before you. You are also connected to the leaders who will follow you. You are leaving your leadership legacy this very minute.

Legacies are the gifts, memories, or images of how leaders are remembered after their leadership days are over. Legacies can be positive and provide models that improve or enhance current practice, or they can cause harm and destruction. Some of the best leadership lessons learned have come from watching ineffective leaders falter. Just as you cannot walk through deep snow without leaving tracks, you cannot lead your school without leaving your legacy behind. Just as you cannot stand in the sun without casting a shadow, you cannot serve without having some level of impact on others.

Table 6.1: Low-, Medium-, and High-Risk Teacher Leadership Opportunities

Low-Risk Teacher Leadership Opportunities	Medium-Risk Teacher Leadership Opportunities	High-Risk Teacher Leadership Opportunities
• Take an active role in curriculum meetings.	• Advocate for your profession.*	• Lead an academy, house, or small learning community.
• Attend brown bag lunches or leadership lunches.	• Attend an in-depth institute in a content area.*	• Participate in committee work at the district, state, provincial, or national level.
• Attend leadership development programs.	• Lead professional learning opportunities.	• Make cross-functional job moves.
• Attend professional learning opportunities.	• Attend school board meetings, workshops, and so on.	• Be a department chair, grade-level chair, or team leader.
• Attend webinars.*	• Be a mentor.*	• Be a district resource teacher or content expert.
• Be mentored.*	• Be a book reviewer.	• Give presentations at conferences.*
• Be observed and receive feedback.	• Coach a colleague.*	• Be an International Baccalaureate coordinator or program leader.
• Become a committee member.	• Become a committee chair or co-chair.	• Take on an increased scope of responsibility.
• Engage in community organization or community service.	• Conduct action research.*	• Lead a schoolwide project or committee.
• Get Crisis Prevention Institute certification (nonviolent crisis intervention training).*	• Consult an expert.	• Lead a team project or assignment.
• Engage in a cycle of inquiry with a team.*	• Create new teaching resources.*	• Lead committees at all levels.
• Examine student data.*	• Provide customized in-house professional learning activities.	• Lead leadership development programs.
• Write grants.	• Become a department co-chair.	• Take on leadership of quality initiatives—Six Sigma, DMAIC, Sterling, Baldrige, and so on.
• Take on an increased scope of responsibility (for example, pursue a stretch goal).	• Develop team facilitation skills.*	• Take on a leadership role in the school improvement planning (SIP) process.
• Join a professional network.	• Do a classroom or school walkthrough.*	• Become a National Board–certified teacher.
• Join an online or face-to-face network.*	• Enroll in a university course.*	• Pursue additional certifications or degrees.*
• Keep a reflective blog or journal.*	• Participate in professional learning from external groups.	• Be a supervising teacher for student interns.
• Learn with the support of a coach.*	• Become a facilitator or co-facilitator.	
• Maintain a professional portfolio.*	• Become a grade-level co-chair.	
• Become a member of a data team.	• Take on an increased scope of responsibility.	
• Become a member of academies, institutes, summits, and so on.	• Invite colleagues to observe you.*	
• Observe a model lesson.*	• Become involved in the school advisory committee, the PTA, the PTO, and so on.	
	• Join a cadre of in-school or in-district trainers.*	

- Participate in a Twitter chat.*
- Participate in a lesson study.*
- Plan lessons with colleagues.*
- Read journals, magazines, blogs, and books.*
- Shadow a student, a teacher, or another professional in the field.*
- Study content standards for your state or province.*
- Use a tuning protocol to examine student work.
- Record your own teaching.*
- Visit another school.

- Make lateral job moves within the school or district.
- Lead a book study.*
- Lead a data team.
- Lead a team project or assignment.
- Lead brown bag lunches or leadership lunches.
- Lead webinars.*
- Become a member of the guiding coalition.
- Be a multigrade teacher.
- Participate in a critical friends (professional support) group.*
- Participate in school-improvement planning.*
- Be a public advocate for students, education, or policy.
- Serve as a substitute dean or assistant principal.
- Serve as a trainer or co-trainer.
- Take on a special in-house assignment.
- Take on a special project.
- Sponsor school clubs.
- Submit articles to professional publications.
- Supervise school activities (such as prom, homecoming, or sports activities).
- Engage in team projects.
- Volunteer at district offices and schools.
- Work with a professional mentor.
- Write an article about your work.*
- Write assessments with colleagues.*

Source for starred leadership opportunities: Learning Forward, 2016.

You are in charge of how your story goes. Will the differences you make be positive, or will they be negative? Do you want others to write your leadership legacy, or do you want to take control and write your own biography?

Many leaders make the mistake of building a résumé rather than creating a legacy. Résumé building is personal; it benefits one person—the leader. Legacy building is interpersonal and benefits the entire organization (Sanborn, 2014). Table 6.2 compares résumé-building skills with legacy-building skills. Are you bolstering your résumé or leaving a path of excellence for others to follow?

Table 6.2: Résumé-Building Skills Versus Legacy-Building Skills

Are You Building Your Résumé With . . . ?	Are You Building Your Legacy With . . . ?
Your accomplishments	Your contributions
The results of your work	The relationships you have made with others
The amount of money you have made	The differences you have made
The impressions you have left	The impact you have left
Your career	Your organization, family, and community
What you have learned	What you have taught
The improvements you have made in yourself	The improvements you have helped others make in themselves

Source: Sanborn, 2014.

The following list offers some strategies for leaving a legacy of positive leadership. Your greatest leverage point is how you assemble and lead your guiding coalition (Bestow Team, 2019; Fanning, 2016).

- **Prioritize people over results:** The primary goal of a PLC is to improve the learning for all students. The means through which you can reach that lofty goal are your faculty and staff.

- **Set your cultural foundation:** When starting the PLC process, your guiding coalition must first develop and mature as a collaborative team before it can begin to pursue the high-altitude work of improving student learning. Your cultural foundation will need to be set first and your collaborative team members will need to develop trust among themselves before they begin sharing their data, results, assessments, and so on. Teams that focus on creating and using their norms, accountability protocols, agendas, and so on will set the stage for working together as a team. By creating a system that focuses on how they work together first, with an emphasis on relationships and trust, your collaborative teams will be better prepared to work together in making data-driven decisions. When you invest your resources in the people with whom you work, the results of their collective efforts will pay handsome dividends.

- **Make personal connections:** As discussed in chapter 2 (page 37) and chapter 4 (page 87), the members of your guiding coalition have lives outside of school. They are spouses, partners, parents, brothers, sisters, grandchildren, and more. Take time to ask about the people they love, the activities they enjoy, and their passions in life. Once your team members respond to how much you listen and care, they will likely make similar connections with members of their collaborative teams. As a result of these personal and interpersonal connections, your PLC's culture will stand a good chance of living on beyond your time in the principalship.

- **Empower staff more, control them less:** Becoming a PLC is risky. When moving to collaborative practices, teachers risk leaving the safety of working in isolation. Teachers who have taken pride in their independence risk sharing knowledge and strategies with colleagues. They risk opening up to others. They can feel afraid in being vulnerable. As principal, you, too, take risks when encouraging your guiding coalition and teams to learn and work interdependently. By easing up on the reins and allowing your teams to learn to become more self-sufficient by working together, you will be providing them with tremendous empowering opportunities. Your guiding coalition members can help reduce risks and fear as they learn and apply PLC practices. Letting go of ineffective practices can open up new and exciting opportunities for your staff to learn and grow.

- **Model the behaviors you expect:** What you do speaks louder than what you say. Everyone is looking to you for direction. How well your guiding coalition is organized and operates is a direct reflection of your leadership. How well your teacher teams are organized and work together is a reflection of how well your guiding coalition applies what it has learned. When you see behaviors that contradict the school's mission, vision, values, and goals, don't just tell staff members how to act; show them.

- **Coach your leaders:** The PLC process gives you and your teams immeasurable opportunities to learn and lead. To create a self-sustaining collaborative culture, start with your guiding coalition. When you see effective practice, give feedback that will encourage your leaders to continue. When you see ineffective practice, coach your learning leaders with best practices.

- **Focus on everyday interactions:** Each day presents innumerable opportunities to lead and model. You do not have to pull teams together to tell them how to work together or how to act. From the minute you arrive at school in the morning, your leadership is evident to every student, teacher, staff member, and parent you pass. It's not the big school rallies, faculty meetings, or professional learning presentations where you showcase your leadership. The power of your leadership is found in small personal interactions, body language, and encouraging words. Examples of these daily interactions include going through the cafeteria during breakfast to welcome students and wish them a good day, taking time to check in with a teacher assistant whose spouse is in the hospital, following up with a student who had a difficult day yesterday, standing with the crossing guard after school to tell him or her how much you appreciate all that he or she has done to ensure students are safe, and so on. Through everyday interactions, you model how much you care about your school community.

- **Advocate for younger employees:** When creating your guiding coalition, be sure to consider assembling as diverse a team as possible. Depending on the most experienced personnel to lead your teams has advantages, but if yours is to be a learning culture, younger staff members bring much to the table. For example, their strengths lie in current best practice, new perspectives, and application of the newest technology. Perhaps many younger teachers are not ready for higher risk leadership responsibilities; however, they certainly can serve in leadership support roles, such as in a committee co-chair, recorder, or co-presenter role during professional learning sessions.

- **Be a positive mentor:** Leading a guiding coalition and a PLC takes time and patience. Guiding coalition members look to you for trust and advice as they move through the process to lead their teams. Your availability and support are essential. Staying positive and keeping their best interests at heart will go a long way to giving them the guidance and confidence they need to succeed.

Carol Dweck (2016) reminds leaders that many people's lives are in their trust. Teachers and staff are principals' responsibility and legacy. The language and actions that flow from the growth mindset can help you fulfill your mission as a principal. The legacy you leave can help your employees fulfill their potential.

Conclusion

All the levers of leadership this chapter has discussed center on the relationships you have with those whom you lead. Applying these levers helps facilitate your school's journey to becoming a PLC. Over time, your leadership levers will lengthen and strengthen. Leveraging your leadership creates and sustains effective PLC practices. Each time you apply these levers, you elevate those with whom you work. The result of leading through your guiding coalition will ultimately be a sustainable and self-sufficient culture of excellence.

▶ Next Steps ▶

Think about the leaders, mentors, and coaches who have guided and encouraged you along your leadership journey. These leaders can be individuals in the profession, individuals outside the profession, family, friends—anyone who has positively impacted you and helped shape the leader you are today. Included in your list might be individuals whom you have never met. They might be authors, politicians, musicians, or clergy members.

Use figure 6.2 as you reflect on who has impacted you and helped mold the leader you are today. List the admirable leadership qualities, characteristics, or traits that each person exhibits. Are there commonalities among the traits? Are there many singleton traits, where only one person has those particular qualities? Reflect on your leadership qualities and traits. What do you consider to be your greatest strengths? After looking at the overall qualities of those who have helped you along the way, do you see yourself as the sum of all their traits? Are you passing on their leadership legacies to others? If not, how might you make those traits part of your legacy?

Which individuals have impacted my leadership style?	Which of their characteristics or traits do I admire?	Which of those characteristics or traits do I wish to add to my legacy?	What will I do to ensure each of those characteristics or traits becomes part of my legacy?

FIGURE 6.2: My leadership legacy.

*Visit **go.SolutionTree.com/PLCbooks** for a free reproducible version of this figure.*

? FAQs

I have exemplary teachers who will do whatever it takes for our school to become a PLC. A couple of them are even on track to getting their principal's licenses. They are excited about where they are going in their careers. I worry their excitement will turn others off. How do I recruit the reluctant teachers who are turned off by the enthusiastic go-getters? How do I keep the amazing teachers on my staff when others talk behind their backs and refer to them as the principal's pets and goody-two-shoes teachers?

You touch on a common concern that many of your colleagues share. In his book *Dealing With Difficult Teachers*, Todd Whitaker (2015) identifies three distinct teacher types: (1) superstars, (2) backbones, and (3) mediocres. Your question describes the results of relationships among the superstars and the mediocres. Superstar teachers will embrace the PLC concepts. They are motivated and enthusiastic about improving student learning. The mediocres are stuck in the past and generally fear change and disruption to their routine. Any change can cause anxiety and a negative response. However, the complete cultural transformation found in becoming a PLC is usually more than they can handle. They typically fear how they will fit into the new environment. There's safety in staying in the past.

Generally, principals spend more time and effort dealing with the mediocres and far less time and effort working with the superstars. Whitaker's (2015) approach to dealing with these different styles is to invest the majority of your resources in supporting and growing the skills of the superstars and the effective and solid teachers, the backbones. Then deal with the mediocres using various situational strategies, which may include:

- Minimize their influence on other teachers, especially newer staff members
- Confront them about their observable behaviors
- Assume they want to do what is right
- Treat them with respect
- Look for opportunities to catch them doing something right
- Praise them publicly
- Raise their level of discomfort by using peer pressure

Most of my staff are not interested in being leaders or taking on responsibilities outside the classroom. They are good, solid, hardworking professionals. Most just want to be good teachers and let me lead the school. How can I create leadership capacity when I can't even seem to generate interest in taking on leadership responsibilities?

No principal wants to lead a school that turns out assistant principals and principals by the dozen, like a factory might. Your faculty describes most faculties in schools today: solid, hardworking, and passionate about students. These traits are needed in a PLC. To many teachers, *leadership* is a frightening term that can mean risk, failure, added responsibility, less time teaching, and so on. If you know your teachers fear the term *leadership*, then steer clear of using it.

When starting work with your guiding coalition, focus on the why of becoming a PLC—increased learning for all students. That's the hook! Then tell the guiding coalition, "How do we accomplish that learning? We work together through four critical questions in our collaborative teams. These teams will be facilitated by a teacher from each team or department. We will measure the progress of each team by the products required of the work." Ease into the work, and recognize the positive gains made along the way. Be encouraging. Doing so can create capacity without making it the main thing.

Some schools focus exclusively on leadership to the point that it drives everything. However, there are also schools like yours that use a kinder, gentler approach. Every school must meet its own needs to get the work done. Meet your staff where they are, and move on from there.

I have teachers who cannot say no to anything. They get overcommitted and overloaded in their leadership roles. I worry they are going to burn out. What should I do?

You may wish to look at the distribution of leadership in your school. Is it equitable? Is every member of your staff contributing to some degree? If some are still on the sidelines, you may try to get them involved by giving them parts of the leadership workload of those teachers you are concerned about. Redistributing some responsibilities to those not participating may help lower your concerns about overextending certain teacher leaders.

I love the concept of the courageous follower. It makes so much sense to have a critical friend who can close my office door and tell me straight up what's going on. I currently do not have anyone on staff who has been comfortable enough to approach me about how things are going. My challenge is how do I recruit someone for the role? How do I keep others from seeing the person with this role as an insider, my favorite, or a snitch?

The courageous follower role can be as formal or informal as you want it to be. If you are concerned about how others might perceive the role, you might consider offering the role to the entire guiding coalition. Of course, everything hinges on your leadership style and the level of trust you have with your guiding coalition. You also have to consider your willingness to take bad news and criticism. It sounds as if you will view the role as a positive PLC leadership lever, so you might consider sharing the dimensions of courageous followership (see figure 6.1, page 129) with your guiding coalition and seeing how receptive members would be to collectively assuming those responsibilities. If you see the role as a valuable leadership tool and treat it as such, using the role in this way may prove helpful.

Reflection

Review the levers of leadership. Which lever is your strongest? What evidence do you have to support your choice? Which leadership levers do you want to invest resources in to strengthen them? Complete the "Action Plan for Strengthening Leadership Levers" (page 140) to assist you in identifying and strengthening your leadership levers.

Action Plan for Strengthening Leadership Levers

Leadership Levers	Is this leadership lever an area of strength or an area of weakness? What evidence supports your choice?	What actions do you plan to take to strengthen this leadership lever?	What evidence would indicate that your efforts made a difference?
Lead the learning.			
Develop courageous followers.			
Harness the potential and power of teacher leadership.			
Create a legacy of leadership.			

EPILOGUE
A Call to Action

An idea not coupled with action will never get
any bigger than the brain cell it occupied.

—Arnold Glasow

This is a tale of two schools. They had the same grade levels, and they had about the same number of students. The demographics were almost identical. The schools had approximately the same percentages of students on free or reduced meals, English learners, and special education students. Although the schools were very similar in every way, one school outperformed the other across the board. The achievement rate of the first school was almost two and a half times the achievement rate of the second school.

The principal of the second school remarked, "If our schools are so similar, why is our school not performing as well as the other? I know of no staff that works as hard as our staff. Our teachers care deeply about their students. They get along with each other. As principal, I have done everything I can think of, yet our student achievement data are not improving. Why?"

Exasperated, the principal of the second school finally called the principal of the first school. "We've known each other for quite a while; for the longest time, our students achieved about the same results on district and state assessments. But over the past few years, your results have sharply risen while ours have stayed flat. What on earth is in the water over there for your school to achieve the results you've been getting? Did you get a big grant or special funding?"

The principal of the first school replied, "Nope."

"Were your school boundaries redrawn, bringing in higher-achieving students?"

"Nope."

"Have you undergone a major turnover in staff and hired better teachers?"

"Nope."

"New building? New technology?"

"Nope. Nope."

"OK, I give up. What's made the difference?"

"Our teachers have been working in collaborative teams as part of our effort to become a PLC. We have changed absolutely nothing except how we work together to increase student learning. Like you, we were beating our heads against the wall, trying everything under the sun to improve learning. Nothing we tried worked. You know that saying, 'When the horse dies, dismount'? We dismounted. We learned about a research-based process called PLCs at Work, created a powerful guiding coalition to lead our collaborative teacher teams, and dedicated all our efforts and resources toward ensuring high levels of learning for all our students."

The principal of the second school asked, "Can we meet sometime this week? I'd like to buy you lunch and learn more about what your school is doing."

Stories like the first school's have helped many schools take that first step to learn about the PLC process and what it takes to lead it. These stories function as calls to action for schools to take the PLC journey. Making the journey, however, can be long and laborious if these schools have no outside resources and support along the way. For this reason, I have chosen to wrap up this book with a nod to collaboration that can happen beyond the physical walls of your school.

The first school and second school in the opening story were physically close to each other. You might not have the benefit of a school right next door that has had great success in becoming a PLC. Fortunately, there are websites for PLC leaders at all stages of implementation that offer the support of veteran leaders who have been there and done that.

I recommend that you and your guiding coalition access the many free resources on the AllThingsPLC website (www.allthingsPLC.info) and in the free resources menu on the Solution Tree website (www.SolutionTree.com). These websites provide articles and research, tools and resources, a blog and community forum for real-time assistance, free reproducibles, study guides, and other resources, all of which can support you and your teams as you work toward creating a collaborative culture.

To learn about what Model PLC schools have done to achieve the results they have gotten, use the PLC Locator (www.allthingsplc.info/plc-locator/us). It provides current information on schools and districts that have built successful PLCs. To be recognized as a Model PLC, schools must do the following:

- Demonstrate a commitment to the PLC at Work process.

- Implement those concepts for at least three years.

- Present clear evidence of improved student learning.

- Explain the culture, practices, and structures of the school or district, and submit it for consideration to the PLC Review Committee using [the] online submission process.

- Update school or district information on the site each year to show [their] data continue to meet the criteria of the PLC at Work process. (AllThingsPLC, n.d.)

Districts with a district-level guiding coalition may also wish to access AllThingsPLC as well as the free resources menu on the Solution Tree website for resources and expert advice. These resources can prove very helpful in supporting your guiding coalition as it leads your district's PLC process. Strong PLC districts usually have different levels of support and assistance to help school-level guiding coalitions lead their collaborative teams.

Consider having your guiding coalition members discuss what resources they need to access to support the team's current efforts. Then assign sections of AllThingsPLC and the free resources menu on the Solution Tree website to your team members; working in pairs is helpful. Have them use figure E.1 (page 144) as a tool for the review. When the pairs are done with their reviews, have each pair present its findings to the rest of the guiding coalition.

To paraphrase T. S. Eliot (1943), we shall not cease from learning; and the end of all our learning will be to arrive where we started and know the place for the first time. That, too, is my wish for you as you continue your journey to build a powerful guiding coalition to lead your PLC. When moving from thought to action, from learning to doing, consider the following questions.

- How will you share the why for having a more powerful guiding coalition with your school-based leaders?

- How do you plan for your leaders to become more knowledgeable about what a guiding coalition is and what distinguishes its role and responsibilities from those of traditionally organized administrative teams or leadership teams?

- What will your guiding coalition do to ensure faithful implementation of the PLC concepts in order to create and sustain a strong foundation that supports the PLC structure?

- How will your guiding coalition make relationships a top priority in your transformation efforts?

- What will you do to strengthen the collaborative leadership potential among the members of your guiding coalition?

- How will your guiding coalition leverage its leadership to ensure capacity building and sustainability are embedded in your PLC culture?

Instructions for the principal: You and your team members will each need to create accounts to sign in and access the free resources on AllThingsPLC (www.allthingsplc.info) and www.SolutionTree.com.

Familiarize your guiding coalition with the major elements and features of the AllThingsPLC home page. Show the participants the drop-down menus. Do not open the drop-down links. Your teams of two will be exploring those links. Depending on the size of your team, you may need to increase your teams of two or create several teams of three.

Give your teams of two the following website assignments. (Note: These are suggested team assignments. You may design your team assignments to meet your specific needs.)

- Team 1: Blog and the Community drop-down menu and the About drop-down menu

- Team 2: The Articles & Research drop-down menu

- Team 3: The Tools & Resources drop-down menu

- Team 4: The See the Evidence drop-down menu (except for the PLC Locator)

- Teams 5 and 6: The PLC Locator (in the See the Evidence drop-down menu)

The next two teams will review the reproducibles and study guides found under the Free Resources drop-down menu at www.SolutionTree.com.

- Team 7: Open the professional learning communities link found at www.solutiontree.com/free-resources/plcbooks

- Team 8: Open the leadership link found at www.solutiontree.com/free-resources/leadership

Instructions for the guiding coalition:

For the next thirty to forty-five minutes, explore your assigned sections of the AllThingsPLC website and www.SolutionTree.com. What are three key features of your assigned sections?

1.

2.

3.

What features do you believe would benefit your guiding coalition or collaborative teams the most? Why?

In three to five minutes, briefly summarize your findings to the rest of the guiding coalition. Show the pages and features that you are sharing.

After all team summaries, the principal will wrap up the session.

FIGURE E.1: AllThingsPLC processing guide for the guiding coalition.

*Visit **go.SolutionTree.com/PLCbooks** for a free reproducible version of this figure.*

REFERENCES AND RESOURCES

Aczel, K., Roebuck, R., & Wolstencroft, E. (2017). Distributive leadership: Creating teacher leaders, developing collective efficacy and enhancing community voice. In Australian Council for Educational Research (Ed.), *Excellence in Professional Practice Conference 2017: Case studies of practice* (pp. 75–80). Camberwell, Victoria, Australia: Australian Council for Educational Research.

Aldeman, C. (2020, May 18). *Employee benefits continue to take higher and higher share of school district budgets* [Blog post]. Accessed at www.teacherpensions.org/blog/employee-benefits-continue-take -higher-and-higher-share-school-district-budgets on January 27, 2021.

AllAuthor. (n.d.). *David Allan Coe quotes.* Accessed at https://allauthor.com/quotes/8726 on January 27, 2021.

AllThingsPLC. (n.d.). *Apply to be a Model PLC.* Accessed at www.allthingsplc.info/evidence-submission -online on January 28, 2021.

Anderson, J. (2017, April 28). *Fixed vs growth: Two ends of a mindset continuum* [Blog post]. Accessed at https://mindfulbydesign.com/fixed-vs-growth-two-ends-mindset-continuum on January 27, 2021.

Barth, R. S. (2001). *Learning by heart.* San Francisco: Jossey-Bass.

Bennis, W., & Nanus, B. (2007). *Leaders: The strategies for taking charge.* New York: Harper & Row.

Best Life Editors. (2020, February 4). *25 things that have different names throughout the U.S.* Accessed at https://bestlifeonline.com/things-have-different-names-u-s on January 28, 2021.

Bestow Team. (2019, April 1). *How to leave a lasting legacy* [Blog post]. Accessed at www.bestow.com /blog/how-to-leave-a-lasting-legacy on January 27, 2021.

Bhuiyan, T. (n.d.). *Difference between footing and foundation.* Accessed at https://civiltoday.com /geotechnical-engineering/foundation-engineering/219-difference-between-footing-and-foundation on January 27, 2021.

Blankstein, A. M., Houston, P. D., & Cole, R. W. (Eds.). (2008). *Sustaining professional learning communities.* Thousand Oaks, CA: Corwin Press.

Bosworth, P. (n.d.). *How to empower employees in the workplace—8 tips.* Accessed at https:// leadershipchoice.com/empower-employees-in-the-workplace on January 27, 2021.

Bowgren, L., & Sever, K. (2010). *Differentiated professional development in a professional learning community.* Bloomington, IN: Solution Tree Press.

BrainMass. (n.d.). *Does empowerment imply a loss of control in an organization?* [Blog post]. Accessed at https://brainmass.com/business/business-management/empowerment-loss-control -organization-216635 on May 31, 2021.

Bryk, A., & Schneider, B. (2002). *Trust in schools: A core resource for improvement.* New York: Russell Sage Foundation.

Buffum, A. (2008). Trust: The secret ingredient to successful shared leadership. In A. Buffum, C. Erkens, C. Hinman, S. Huff, L. G. Jessie, T. L. Martin, et al., *The collaborative administrator: Working together as a professional learning community* (pp. 55–71). Bloomington, IN: Solution Tree Press.

Buffum, A., Erkens, C., Hinman, C., Huff, S., Jessie, L. G., Martin, T. L., et al. (2008). *The collaborative administrator: Working together as a professional learning community*. Bloomington, IN: Solution Tree Press.

Buffum, A., Mattos, M., & Malone, J. (2018). *Taking action: A handbook for RTI at Work*. Bloomington, IN: Solution Tree Press.

Buffum, A., Mattos, M., & Weber, C. (2012). *Simplifying response to intervention: Four essential guiding principles*. Bloomington, IN: Solution Tree Press.

Burgin, M., & Meissner, G. (2017). 1 + 1 = 3: Synergy arithmetic in economics. *Applied Mathematics*, *8*(2), 133–144. Accessed at https://scirp.org/journal/paperinformation.aspx?paperid=73964 on January 27, 2021.

Carlisle Community Schools. (n.d.). *Guiding coalitions*. Accessed at www.carlislecsd.org/apps/pages /index.jsp?uREC_ID=701701&type=d&pREC_ID=1179878 on January 27, 2021.

Casali, E. (2015, May 9). *A framework for thinking about systems change*. Accessed at https:// intenseminimalism.com/2015/a-framework-for-thinking-about-systems-change on January 27, 2021.

Chaleff, I. (2009). *The courageous follower: Standing up to and for our leaders* (3rd ed.). San Francisco: Berrett-Koehler.

Collins, J. (2001). *Good to great: Why some companies make the leap . . . and others don't* [Kindle ed.]. New York: Harper Business.

Commitment. (n.d.). In *YourDictionary online dictionary*. Accessed at www.yourdictionary.com /commitment on June 4, 2021.

Conlow, R. (2017, May 6). *12 eloquent leading by example quotes* [Blog post]. Accessed at http:// rickconlow.com/12-eloquent-leading-by-example-quotes on January 27, 2021.

Conzemius, A. E., & O'Neill, J. (2014). *The handbook for SMART school teams: Revitalizing best practices for collaboration* (2nd ed.). Bloomington, IN: Solution Tree Press.

Couros, G. (2018, July 24). *Moving beyond a "growth mindset"* [Blog post]. Accessed at https:// georgecouros.ca/blog/archives/8389 on January 27, 2021.

Covey, S. R. (1989). *The seven habits of highly effective people: Restoring the character ethic*. New York: Simon & Schuster.

Covey, S. R. (2020). *The seven habits of highly effective people: Powerful lessons in purposeful change* (Revised and updated ed.). New York: Simon & Schuster.

Department for Professional Employees. (2019). *School administrators: An occupational overview*. Accessed at www.dpeaflcio.org/factsheets/school-administrators-an-occupational-overview on January 27, 2021.

Diplo Learning Corner. (2015, March 24). *The bus metaphor* [Blog post]. Accessed at http://diplolearn .org/2015/03/24/the-bus-metaphor on January 27, 2021.

Doseck, K. (2015, March 27). *Change management: Step 2—Build a guiding coalition*. Accessed at https://viralsolutions.net/change-management-step-2-build-a-guiding-coalition/#.XZdN-EZKiUl on January 27, 2021.

DuFour, R. (2015). *School structures: Traditional school, pseudo-PLC, and PLC* [Presentation handout].

DuFour, R., & DuFour, R. (2006). *An audit of our commitment to key PLC concepts* [Presentation handout].

DuFour, R., DuFour, R., & Eaker, R. (2008). *Revisiting Professional Learning Communities at Work: New insights for improving schools*. Bloomington, IN: Solution Tree Press.

DuFour, R., DuFour, R., Eaker, R., & Karhanek, G. (2010). *Raising the bar and closing the gap: Whatever it takes*. Bloomington, IN: Solution Tree Press.

DuFour, R., DuFour, R., Eaker, R., Many, T. W., & Mattos, M. (2016). *Learning by doing: A handbook for Professional Learning Communities at Work* (3rd ed.). Bloomington, IN: Solution Tree Press.

DuFour, R., DuFour, R., Eaker, R., Mattos, M., & Muhammad, A. (2021). *Revisiting Professional Learning Communities at Work: Proven insights for sustained, substantive school improvement* (2nd ed.). Bloomington, IN: Solution Tree Press.

DuFour, R., & Eaker, R. (1998). *Professional Learning Communities at Work: Best practices for enhancing student achievement.* Bloomington, IN: Solution Tree Press.

DuFour, R., & Fullan, M. (2013). *Cultures built to last: Systemic PLCs at Work.* Bloomington, IN: Solution Tree Press.

DuFour, R., & Marzano, R. J. (2011). *Leaders of learning: How district, school, and classroom leaders improve student achievement.* Bloomington, IN: Solution Tree Press.

Dweck, C. S. (2016). *Mindset: The new psychology of success* (Updated ed.). New York: Random House.

Eaker, R., DuFour, R., & DuFour, R. (2002). *Getting started: Reculturing schools to become professional learning communities.* Bloomington, IN: Solution Tree Press.

Eaker, R., Hagadone, M., Keating, J., & Rhoades, M. (2021). *Leading PLCs at Work districtwide: From boardroom to classroom.* Bloomington, IN: Solution Tree Press.

Easton, L. B. (2011). *Professional learning communities by design: Putting the learning back into PLCs.* Thousand Oaks, CA: Corwin Press.

Eaton, S. (2011). *The 3rd alternative.* Accessed at https://huntsman.usu.edu/news/magazine/pdfs /2011Fall.pdf on June 2, 2021.

Elephant trap. (n.d.). In *Wiktionary.* Accessed at https://en.wiktionary.org/wiki/elephant_trap #:~:text=elephant%20trap%20(plural%20elephant%20traps,set%20him%20an%20elephant %20trap on September 24, 2020.

Eliot, T. S. (1943). *Four quartets.* New York: Harcourt.

Ellerson, N. (n.d.). *School budgets 101.* Accessed at https://aasa.org/uploadedFiles/Policy_and _Advocacy/files/SchoolBudgetBriefFINAL.pdf on January 27, 2021.

Ellifritz, G. (2014, September 30). *"Aim small, hit small" shooting drill* [Blog post]. Accessed at www .activeresponsetraining.net/aim-small-hit-small-shooting-drill on January 27, 2021.

Empowerment. (n.d.). In *Merriam-Webster's online dictionary.* Accessed at www.merriam-webster.com /dictionary/empowerment on January 28, 2021.

Erkens, C., & Twadell, E. (2012). *Leading by design: An action framework for PLC at Work leaders.* Bloomington, IN: Solution Tree Press.

Fanning, B. (2016, November 18). 5 ways the best leaders leave unforgettable legacies: How your legacy can last at work. *Inc.* Accessed at www.inc.com/ben-fanning/5-ways-the-best-leaders-leave -unforgettable-legacies.html on January 27, 2021.

Ferrabee, D. (2016, February 29). *5 change management rules for building a world-class guiding coalition.* Accessed at www.managers.org.uk/insights/news/2016/february/change-management-5 -rules-for-building-a-world-class-guiding-coalition on January 27, 2021.

Firth, G. R. (1976). Theories of leadership: Where do we stand? *Educational Leadership, 33*(5), 327–331. Accessed at www.ascd.org/ASCD/pdf/journals/ed_lead/el_197602_firth.pdf on January 27, 2021.

FranklinCovey. (2017, August 24). *Big rocks* [Video file]. Accessed at www.youtube.com/watch ?v=zV3gMTOEWt8&list=PLjBezK36_-v0DLphSXAHnJVd_5gEaQDjK on January 27, 2021.

Frazer, J. (2018, January 11). *A simple explanation of the BE DO HAVE model* [Blog post]. Accessed at http://jaeminfrazer.com/blog/a-simple-explanation-of-the-be-do-have-model on January 27, 2021.

Froehlich, M. (2019, October 9). *Hierarchy of needs for innovation & divergent thinking: Mindset.* Accessed at: https://mandyfroehlich.com/2017/12/10/hierarchy-of-needs-for-innovation-divergent-thinking-mindset/ on May 5, 2021.

Fullan, M. (2003). *The moral imperative of school leadership.* Thousand Oaks, CA: Corwin Press.

Fullan, M. (2006). *Facilitator's guide, leadership and sustainability: System thinkers in action.* Thousand Oaks, CA: Corwin Press.

Galloway, D. (2019, July 22). *Leverage opinion leaders to make change happen.* Accessed at www.continuousmile.com/leadership/leverage-opinion-leaders-to-make-change-happen on January 27, 2021.

Garn, T. (2010, June 30). *Be-do-have* [Blog post]. Accessed at http://tanyagarn.blogspot.com/2010/06/be-do-have.html on January 28, 2021.

Goeres, E. (2017, February 1). *What does a car's alternator do?* Accessed at www.thedrive.com/tech/7298/what-does-a-cars-alternator-do on January 27, 2021.

Goin, D. (2012, February 8). Guiding coalition: A dream team to help you implement strategy quickly. *Forbes.* Accessed at www.forbes.com/sites/johnkotter/2012/02/08/guiding-coalition-a-dream-team-to-help-you-implement-strategy-quickly/?sh=b4d3524b294a on April 19, 2021.

Goodreads. (n.d.). *Benjamin Franklin quotes.* Accessed at www.goodreads.com/quotes/247269-an-ounce-of-prevention-is-worth-a-pound-of-cure on January 27, 2021.

Hall, B. (2008). Keep the leadership pipeline flowing. *Journal of Staff Development, 29*(3), 33–36.

Hall, B. (2012, March 14). *Creating and supporting high-performing PLCs: One district's journey* [Blog post]. Accessed at www.allthingsplc.info/blog/view/172/creating-and-supporting-high-performing-plcs-one-districtrsquos-journey on April 26, 2021.

Hall, B. (2018, Spring). Want successful PLCs? Effective leadership matters most. *AllThingsPLC Magazine,* 14–20.

Hall, P., & Simeral, A. (2019, April 15). *Stop, practice, collaborate: The cycle of reflective teaching.* Accessed at www.teachthought.com/pedagogy/the-cycle-of-reflective-teaching on January 27, 2021.

Hargreaves, A., & Fink, D. (2006). *Sustainable leadership.* San Francisco: Jossey-Bass.

Hasa. (2016, July 28). *Difference between group and team.* Accessed at https://pediaa.com/difference-between-group-and-team on January 27, 2021.

Hock, J. (Director). (2013, March 17). Survive and advance [Television series episode]. In P. A. Aromando, J. Dahl, A. Evans, D. Fenton, J. Podhoretz, C. Schell, et al. (Producers), *30 for 30.* Bristol, CT: ESPN Films.

Hoerr, T. R. (2017). Educators need grit too! *Educational Leadership, 74*(9), 60–64. Accessed at www.ascd.org/publications/educational-leadership/summer17/vol74/num09/Educators-Need-Grit-Too!.aspx on January 27, 2021.

Honesty. (n.d.). In *TalkingTree Books online resource.* Accessed at https://talkingtreebooks.com/teaching-resources-catalog//lesson-plans/honesty-lesson-plan-presentation on June 4, 2021.

Hord, S. M., & Sommers, W. A. (2008). *Leading professional learning communities: Voices from research and practice.* Thousand Oaks, CA: Corwin Press.

Interaction Associates. (n.d.). *Meeting facilitation services.* Accessed at www.interactionassociates.com/services/meeting-facilitation on January 27, 2021.

Jackson, J. (2020, January 21). *What is your management-to-leadership ratio?* [Blog post]. Accessed at www.forbes.com/sites/jarretjackson/2020/07/21/what-is-your-management-to-leadership-ratio/?sh=474c2bda741a on June 4, 2021.

James, M. (2012, January 12). *Diffusion of adoption: Using the creative differences* [Blog post]. Accessed at https://creativeemergence.typepad.com/the_fertile_unknown/2012/01/according-to-wikipedia -diffusion-of-innovations-is-a-theory-that-seeks-to-explain-how-why-and-at-what-rate-new-ideas -and-t.html on January 27, 2021.

Jason. (n.d.). *How to build a building foundation—10 steps.* Accessed at https://civilengineersforum .com/how-to-construct-building-foundation on January 27, 2021.

Jones, M., & Silberzahn, P. (2016, March 15). Without an opinion, you're just another person with data. *Forbes.* Accessed at www.forbes.com/sites/silberzahnjones/2016/03/15/without-an-opinion -youre-just-another-person-with-data/#125ddb06699f on January 27, 2021.

Jose, J. (2014). *Groups and teams* [Slideshow]. Accessed at www.slideshare.net/jeshinjose/groups -teams-37536490 on January 27, 2021.

Jukes, I. (2017, December 4). *Why are we called committed sardines?* [Blog post]. Accessed at https:// infosavvy21.com/2017/12/04/why-are-we-called-committed-sardines on January 27, 2021.

Kanold, T. D. (2011). *The five disciplines of PLC leaders.* Bloomington, IN: Solution Tree Press.

Kaplan, L. S., & Owings, W. A. (2013). *Culture re-boot: Reinvigorating school culture to improve student outcomes.* Thousand Oaks, CA: Corwin Press.

Katzenmeyer, M., & Moller, G. (2009). *Awakening the sleeping giant: Helping teachers develop as leaders* (3rd ed.). Thousand Oaks, CA: Corwin Press.

Keating, J., Eaker, R., DuFour, R., & DuFour, R. (2008). *The journey to becoming a professional learning community.* Bloomington, IN: Solution Tree Press.

Kettley, S. (2019, June 19). JFK moon speech: Read President Kennedy's historic Rice 'we choose to go to the moon' speech. *Express.* Accessed at www.express.co.uk/news/science/1142462/JFK-Moon -speech-President-John-F-Kennedy-Rice-we-choose-to-go-Moon-speech-nasa-news on January 28, 2021.

Killion, J., Hord, S. M., Roy, P., Kennedy, J., & Hirsh, S. (2012). *Standards into practice: School-based roles—Innovation configuration maps for standards for professional learning.* Oxford, OH: Learning Forward.

King James Bible. (n.d.). Cleveland, OH: World.

Kotter, J. P. (1996). *Leading change.* Boston: Harvard Business School Press.

Kotter, J. P. (1999). *John P. Kotter on what leaders really do.* Boston: Harvard Business School Press.

Kotter, J. P. (2011, May 24). Building the team you need to drive change. *Forbes.* Accessed at www .forbes.com/sites/johnkotter/2011/05/24/building-the-team-you-need-to-drive-change /#5280c0ec4979 on January 27, 2021.

Kouzes, J. M., & Posner, B. Z. (2017). *The leadership challenge: How to make extraordinary things happen in organizations* (6th ed.). Hoboken, NJ: Wiley.

Kruse, S. D., & Louis, K. S. (2009). *Building strong school cultures: A guide to leading change.* Thousand Oaks, CA: Corwin Press.

Lee, A., Willis, S., & Tian, A. W. (2018, March 2). When empowering employees works, and when it doesn't. *Harvard Business Review.* Accessed at https://hbr.org/2018/03/when-empowering-employees -works-and-when-it-doesnt on April 23, 2021.

Learning Forward. (n.d.a). *Standards for leadership.* Accessed at https://learningforward.org/standards /leadership on April 29, 2021.

Learning Forward. (n.d.b). *Standards for learning communities.* Accessed at https://learningforward.org /standards/learning-communities on April 29, 2021.

Learning Forward. (2016). Beyond the workshop. *Journal of Staff Development, 37*(3), 54–55. Accessed at https://learningforward.org/wp-content/uploads/2016/06/tool-beyond-the-workshop-june16.pdf on January 27, 2021.

Levin, S., & Bradley, K. (n.d.). *Understanding and addressing principal turnover: A review of the research*. Palo Alto, CA: Learning Policy Institute. Accessed at https://learningpolicyinstitute.org/sites/default/files/product-files/NASSP_LPI_Principal_Turnover_Research_Review_REPORT.pdf on January 27, 2021.

Martin, T. L., & Rains, C. L. (2018). *Stronger together: Answering the questions of collaborative leadership*. Bloomington, IN: Solution Tree Press.

Marzano, R. J. (2003). *What works in schools: Translating research into action*. Alexandria, VA: Association for Supervision and Curriculum Development.

Marzano, R. J., Waters, T., & McNulty, B. A. (2005). *School leadership that works: From research to results*. Alexandria, VA: Association for Supervision and Curriculum Development.

Maslow, A. H. (1966). *The psychology of science: A reconnaissance*. New York: Harper & Row.

Mattos, M., DuFour, R., DuFour, R., Eaker, R., & Many, T. W. (2016). *Concise answers to frequently asked questions about Professional Learning Communities at Work*. Bloomington, IN: Solution Tree Press.

McKeever, B., & California School Leadership Academy. (2003). *Nine lessons of successful school leadership teams: Distilling a decade of innovation*. San Francisco: WestEd.

Meg's Milieu. (2012, July). *Reflections: Have, do, be* [Blog post]. Accessed at http://megsmilieu.com/2012/07/have-do-be on January 27, 2021.

Miller, J. (n.d.). *Leaderly quote: When the best leader's work is done . . .* [Blog post]. Accessed at https://beleaderly.com/leaderly-quotes-when-a-leaders-best-work-is-done on January 28, 2021.

Miller, J. (2008, October). *13 lean leadership lessons from Dwight D. Eisenhower* [Blog post]. Accessed at https://blog.gembaacademy.com/2008/10/14/13_lean_leadership_lessons_from_dwight_d_eisenhowe/#:~:text=%2013%20Lean%20Leadership%20Lessons%20from%20Dwight%20D.,safety%20with%20solvency.%20The%20country%20is...%20More%20 on May 31, 2021.

Muhammad, A. (2018). *Transforming school culture: How to overcome staff division* (2nd ed.). Bloomington, IN: Solution Tree Press.

Muhammad, A., & Cruz, L. F. (2019). *Time for change: Four essential skills for transformational school and district leaders*. Bloomington, IN: Solution Tree Press.

Muñoz, M. A., & Branham, K. E. (2016). Professional learning communities focusing on results and data-use to improve student learning: The right implementation matters. *Planning and Changing, 47*(1–2), 37–46.

Mwiya, I. C. (2015, February 11). *The 3-step goal-setting process* [Blog post]. Accessed at https://isaaccmwiya.wordpress.com/2015/02/11/the-3-step-goal-setting-process on April 16, 2021.

Naywinaung, T. (2014). *Leadership and management lesson plan* [Slideshow]. Accessed at www.slideshare.net/ThureinNaywinaung/leadership-and-management-lesson-plan on January 28, 2021.

O'Leary, D. (2016). *Introduction to groups and teams: GE347—Group dynamics*. Accessed at https://view.officeapps.live.com/op/view.aspx?src=https%3A%2F%2Fmrolearysclassroomdotcom.files.wordpress.com%2F2011%2F03%2Fge347-e28093-group-dynamics-week-1.ppt on June 2, 2021.

Page, N., & Czuba, C. E. (1999). Empowerment: What is it? *Journal of Extension, 37*(5), 1–5.

Pearce, D. (2013, November 19). *5 social business adopter types: Prepare early*. Accessed at https://informationweek.com/software/social/5-social-business-adopter-types-prepare-early/d/d-id/898950?piddl_msgorder=asc on January 28, 2021.

Peters, T., & Austin, N. (1985). *A passion for excellence: The leadership difference*. New York: Random House.

Pfeffer, J., & Sutton, R. I. (2000). *The knowing-doing gap: How smart companies turn knowledge into action*. Boston: Harvard Business School Press.

Price, T. (2019, October 7). *Three consequences of no clear organizational vision* [Blog post]. Accessed at www.timpriceblog.com/three-consequences-of-no-clear-organizational-vision on January 28, 2021.

Reeves, D. B. (2006). *The learning leader: How to focus school improvement for better results*. Alexandria, VA: Association for Supervision and Curriculum Development.

Reeves, D. B. (2020). *The learning leader: How to focus school improvement for better results* (2nd ed.). Alexandria, VA: Association for Supervision and Curriculum Development.

Respect. (n.d.). In *WordHippo online dictionary*. Accessed at www.wordhippo.com/what-is/the-noun-for/respect.html on June 4, 2021.

Ribeiro, S. (2020, May 1). *Workplace collaboration: Team vs group* [Blog post]. Accessed at https://blog.flock.com/workplace-collaboration-teams-vs-groups on January 28, 2021.

RightAttitudes.com. (n.d.). *Inspirational quotes by Tom Peters (American management consultant)* [Blog post]. Accessed at https://inspiration.rightattitudes.com/authors/tom-peters/ on May 24, 2021.

Rogers, E. M. (2003). *Diffusion of innovations* (5th ed.). New York: Free Press.

Rooney, J. (2013). For principals: Planning the first year. *Educational Leadership, 70*(9), 73–76. Accessed at www.ascd.org/publications/educational-leadership/summer13/vol70/num09/For-Principals@-Planning-the-First-Year.aspx on January 28, 2021.

Russell, M. (2017, November 23). *Strategic leadership: Managing things and leading people*. Accessed at https://medium.com/swlh/strategic-leadership-managing-things-and-leading-people-2e6b15650870 on January 28, 2021.

Rydell, J. (n.d.). *Show me your calendar and your checkbook, and I'll show you what's really important in your life* [Blog post]. Accessed at https://ducttapemarketing.com/calendar-checkbook on January 28, 2021.

Saddington, J. (2016). *Bad systems and good people* [Blog post]. Accessed at https://john.do/bad-systems-good-people/ on May 24, 2021.

Sahin, I. (2006). Detailed review of Rogers' diffusion of innovations theory and educational technology-related studies based on Rogers' theory. *The Turkish Online Journal of Educational Technology, 5*(2), 14–23. Accessed at http://tojet.net/articles/v5i2/523.pdf on January 28, 2021.

Samur, A. (2019, March 19). *Collaborative leadership: Moving from top-down to team-centric* [Blog post]. Accessed at https://slack.com/blog/collaboration/collaborative-leadership-top-down-team-centric on January 28, 2021.

Sanborn, M. (2014, November 10). *8 differences between your resume and your legacy* [Blog post]. Accessed at https://marksanborn.com/blog/2014/11/10/8-differences-resume-legacy on January 28, 2021.

Sayers, S. (1978). *Leadership styles: A behavioral matrix*. Portland, OR: Northwest Regional Educational Laboratory.

Schmoker, M. (2004). Learning communities at the crossroads: Toward the best schools we've ever had. *Phi Delta Kappan, 86*(1), 84–89.

Sichol, L. B. (2019). *From an idea to Nike: How marketing made Nike a global success*. Boston: Houghton Mifflin Harcourt.

Stephenson, S. (2009). *Leading with trust: How to build strong school teams*. Bloomington, IN: Solution Tree Press.

Stewart, K. (2016, June 2). *Are you a transition person?* Accessed at https://enkindlewellness.com.au/are-you-a-transition-person on January 28, 2021.

Synergy. (n.d.). In *Lexico*. Accessed at www.lexico.com/en/definition/synergy on January 28, 2021.

Tanner, R. (2021, January 25). *Leading change (step 2): Create the guiding coalition*. Accessed at https://managementisajourney.com/leading-change-step-2-create-the-guiding-coalition on January 28, 2021.

Transparency. (n.d.). In *DifferenceBetween online resource*. Accessed at www.differencebetween.com/difference-between-transparency-and-vs-accountability/ on June 4, 2021.

True Colors. (n.d.). *What is True Colors?* Accessed at https://truecolorsintl.com/what-is-true-colors on January 28, 2021.

Trust. (n.d.). In *Merriam-Webster's online dictionary*. Accessed at www.merriam-webster.com/dictionary/trust on June 4, 2021.

Tschannen-Moran, M. (2014). *Trust matters: Leadership for successful schools* (2nd ed.). San Francisco: Jossey-Bass.

Van Clay, M., Soldwedel, P., & Many, T. W. (2011). *Aligning school districts as PLCs*. Bloomington, IN: Solution Tree Press.

Vulnerability. (n.d.). In *Merriam-Webster's online dictionary*. Accessed at www.merriam-webster.com/dictionary/empowerment on June 4, 2021.

Wagner, T., & Kegan, R. (2006). *Change leadership: A practical guide to transforming our schools*. San Francisco: Jossey-Bass.

Walla Walla Public Schools. (n.d.). *WWPS promise standards*. Accessed at www.wwps.org/departments/curriculum/promise-standards on January 28, 2021.

Wallace Foundation. (2013, January). *The school principal as leader: Guiding schools to better teaching and learning* (Expanded ed.). New York: Author. Accessed at www.wallacefoundation.org/knowledge-center/school-leadership/effective-principal-leadership/Documents/The-School-Principal-as-Leader-Guiding-Schools-to-Better-Teaching-and-Learning.pdf on April 19, 2021.

The W. Edwards Deming Institute. (2015, February 26). *A bad system will beat a good person every time* [Blog post]. Accessed at https://blog.deming.org/2015/02/a-bad-system-will-beat-a-good-person-every-time on January 27, 2021.

Welcome, D. (2019, August 1). *Leading as a courageous follower* [Blog post]. Accessed at https://blogs.managementconcepts.com/leading-as-a-courageous-follower on January 28, 2021.

Whitaker, T. (2015). *Dealing with difficult teachers* (3rd ed.). New York: Routledge.

Wilhelm, T. (2017). *Shared leadership: The essential ingredient for effective PLCs*. Thousand Oaks, CA: Corwin Press.

Winter, J. (2017). *Balancing act: Managing vs leading vs coaching*. [Blog post]. Accessed at www.linkedin.com/pulse/balancing-act-managing-vs-leading-coaching-jeff-winter on June 4, 2021.

Young, S. C. (n.d.). *Release the power of Re³*. Accessed at http://susancyoung.com/keynotes/release-the-power-of-re3 on January 28, 2021.

INDEX

big ideas of a PLC and, 41, 43, 44
brainstorming process tool for, 47–48
collaborative culture and, 38, 39, 134
common vocabulary and, 70
critical questions of a PLC and, 44, 47, 48–49
focus on learning and, 41
grade-level or department teams, 99–100
guiding coalitions and, 4, 10
learning, leading the, 127–128
PLC implementation and, 15
PLC leadership teams and, 12
PLC process and, 3
practices for, 28–29
roles of, 32
teacher leadership and, 131
collective commitments. *See also* values
empowerment and, 99
PLC foundations and, 77–79
true PLCs and, 61
Collins, J., 14
common formative assessments, 49
common vocabulary, 66, 70
communication, 110
competency, 94, 96
controllers (gold)
FAQs, 121–122
leadership for all faculty personalities, 115, 116
sample strategies for leading collaboration with different styles, 118
sample styles-planning template, 122
styles-planning template, 124
courageous followers, 24, 128–129, 139
Covey, S., 39, 72
creating a powerful guiding coalition
about, 9–10
application for guiding coalition membership, 24–25
conclusion, 25, 28
FAQs, 29, 32–34
guiding coalition membership, 16–24
next steps, 28–29
PLC leadership teams and, 12, 14
reflections, 34
reproducibles for, 35
teams for PLC implementation and, 14–16
traditional leadership teams and, 11–12
where do we go from here? worksheet, 30–31
credibility, power of, 17
critical questions of a PLC
FAQs, 51–52

leading the four critical questions of a PLC, 44, 47–49
results orientation and, 43
true PLCs and, 61
culture. *See also* collaborative culture and collective responsibility
collaborative culture, 38–39, 42
creating a legacy of leadership and, 134
PLC creation and, 63–65
professional learning and, 131
tool for assessing the initial stages to ensure a strong PLC culture, 82
current reality, 64, 66

D

data teams, use of term. *See* guiding coalitions, 14
data/data analysis
data picture of our school, 67–69
PLC creation and, 66
department heads, 15
design teams, use of term. *See* guiding coalitions, 14
DuFour, R., 4, 93, 126

E

Eaker, R., 4, 93
early adopters, 19, 21, 22
early majority, 19, 21
elephant traps, 23–24
empowerment
about, 98–99
FAQs, 104
meetings and, 99
safety measures and, 100–101
team leadership and, 99–100
values and collective commitments and, 99
essential standards, 47–48
executive teams, use of term. *See* guiding coalitions, 14
expertise, power of, 16–17

F

FAQs
for collaborative leadership, 119–123
for creating a powerful guiding coalition, 29, 32–34
for leading the PLC basics, 51–54
for leveraging your leadership, 137–139
for PLC foundations, 81–84

Learning by Doing, Third Edition
Richard DuFour, Rebecca DuFour, Robert Eaker, Thomas W. Many, and Mike Mattos
Discover how to transform your school or district into a high-performing PLC. The third edition of this comprehensive action guide offers new strategies for addressing critical PLC topics, including hiring and retaining new staff, creating team-developed common formative assessments, and more.
BKF746

Concise Answers to Frequently Asked Questions About Professional Learning Communities at Work®
Mike Mattos, Richard DuFour, Rebecca DuFour, Robert Eaker, and Thomas W. Many
Get all of your PLC questions answered. Designed as a companion resource to *Learning by Doing: A Handbook for Professional Learning Communities at Work®* (3rd ed.), this powerful, quick-reference guidebook is a must-have for teachers and administrators working to create and sustain the PLC process.
BKF705

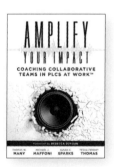

Amplify Your Impact
Thomas W. Many, Michael J. Maffoni, Susan K. Sparks, and Tesha Ferriby Thomas
Now is the time to improve collaboration in your PLC. Using the latest research on coaching and collaboration, the authors share concrete action steps your school can take to adopt proven collaborative coaching methods, fortify teacher teams, and ultimately improve student learning in classrooms.
BKF794

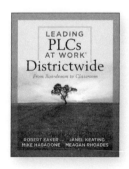

Leading PLCs at Work® Districtwide
Robert Eaker, Mike Hagadone, Janel Keating, and Meagan Rhoades
Ensure your district is doing the right work, the right way, for the right reasons. With this resource as your guide, you will learn how to align the work of every PLC team districtwide—from the boardroom to the classroom.
BKF942

Leading PLCs at Work® Districtwide Plan Book
Robert Eaker, Mike Hagadone, Janel Keating, and Meagan Rhoades
Champion continuous improvement with the support of our *Leading PLCs at Work® Districtwide Plan Book*. Divided into weekly and monthly planning pages, the plan book helps guide leaders in identifying and acting upon major responsibilities, tasks, and goals throughout the year.
BKG004

Solution Tree | Press   *a division of*
Solution Tree

Visit SolutionTree.com or call 800.733.6786 to order.

"Tremendous, tremendous, tremendous!

The speaker made me do some very deep internal reflection about the **PLC process** and the personal responsibility I have in making the school improvement process work **for ALL kids.**"

—Marc Rodriguez, teacher effectiveness coach,
Denver Public Schools, Colorado